INNER PEACE
IN A 9-*to*-5 WORLD

INNER PEACE IN A 9~to~5 WORLD

Attaining Enlightenment Amidst the Chaos

Renata Somogyi

A CITADEL PRESS BOOK
PUBLISHED BY CAROL PUBLISHING GROUP

*This book is dedicated to all those
who are seeking their path along the red road,
with integrity, compassion, and love.*

A Citadel Press Book
Published by Carol Publishing Group
Citadel Press is a registered trademark of Carol Communications, Inc.
Editorial Offices: 600 Madison Avenue, New York, N.Y. 10022
Sales and Distribution Offices: 120 Enterprise Avenue,
Secaucus, N.J. 07094
In Canada: Canadian Manda Group, One Atlantic Avenue, Suite 105,
Toronto, Ontario M6K 3E7
Queries regarding rights and permissions should be addressed to Carol
Publishing Group, 600 Madison Avenue, New York, N.Y. 10022

Manufactured in the United States of America

ISBN 0-8065-1750-6

Contents

Part 3: SOUL

Preface

You are about to enter a world of philosophy, love, physical exercises, and mental stretches. Topics range from food and aromatherapy to yoga and stretching exercises, and include suggestions on ways to fit these into an already full life. The key is: They will not make your life fuller on the outside, where you will now have these extra things to do, but they will make you feel fuller on the *inside*. My goal in offering this book is to help people cope with everyday stresses by learning relaxation techniques—mental and physical—and by learning how to incorporate them into every aspect of daily life.

The topics covered in this book should not be looked at as things you *have to do* to relax; they are merely offered as alternatives that will make a difference. I am not going to promise instant healing if you do these exercises, but I am promising a change in how you feel and how you look at things. You will get as much out of the suggestions in this book as you put in.

We need to open our eyes and see beyond what we can perceive with our five senses. The topics I cover here are not practices and exercises that have been discovered in recent years; these are practices and beliefs that have been in use for thousands of years all over the world.

I am coming to you as a fellow student of this life with a strong desire to help others. If only a handful of people benefit from trying these relaxation techniques, that's fewer people who will be angry, intolerant, and unfocused. Maybe their new calmness, in turn, will help spark some creativity in their own lives or in their environment. Who knows what can happen? We have become an angry society without knowing why we're angry or, in some cases, even that we *are* angry.

I wish you well in the work that lies ahead, and I hope every one of you finds the inner peace you have been longing for.

Acknowledgments

I wish to thank the following: my family for their unconditional love and support through the writing of this book and always; all of the people at Carol Publishing who were involved with this book, in helping to make its transition from a dream to a reality; the men and women in and out of the circles I have been involved with who have offered their guidance, patience, and love to teaching; and finally I wish to thank my guide, guru, and love from many lifetimes, Charlie, who has taught me that things aren't always as they seem, and to peel away the onion.

INTRODUCTION

Looking for Nirvana in All the Wrong Places

Okay, it's 6:30 P.M.; the baby's crying; dinner's burning; your spouse has just called to say he has to work late; this afternoon, just as you were planning to sneak out of the office a few minutes early, your boss came up with some new information that requires you to entirely revise the presentation you were all set to make tomorrow morning; and yesterday's breakfast dishes are piled high in the sink.

You stare wearily at the cover of the latest *Yoga Journal* magazine, which promises ways to cut back on the stresses of your life by showing you how to do a series of ancient yoga stretches recently discovered illustrated on papyrus rolls found in caves near Calcutta.

What the magazine doesn't tell you is how you can find the time to do the stretches when you can't find even five minutes for yourself in your daily two-income-family juggling act that includes in-laws, kids, car pools, traffic jams, meal preparation, household chores, and "quality time" for your spouse and children. Whew! Don't forget to take out the garbage and the dog.

Stresses in our day-to-day lives have reached a critical point for most of us, resulting in a burgeoning movement of people striving to simplify their lives and live closer to nature. Witness the popularity of foods with half the fat, sugar, and chemicals, and the resurgence of handmade household items. Read in the business pages about the success of health-food supermarkets. Note how people are flocking to less congested areas, as if trying to prove to themselves that trees really do exist in the wild and that not all animals are caged.

Over time, stress can produce physical symptoms and contribute to worsening existing conditions such as hypertension. But stress *can* be dealt with successfully. A growing number of studies have shown how powerful are thoughts, emotions, and basic mental health in dealing with stress and maintaining a healthy life.

The practice of homeopathy (which uses small doses of natural remedies) is experiencing a huge comeback as an alternative health measure. It has become the preferred way of treating health problems for many people who no longer want to immediately turn to mainstream allopathic pharmaceutical methods. That the American Medical Association (AMA) takes this as a threat to its livelihood is apparent in its move to try and take vitamins off the shelves, and in its refusal to acknowledge natural therapies as legitimate by fighting the extension of health insurance coverage to include available methods of natural healing.

The AMA and the allopathic pharmaceutical companies probably feel threatened by this shift of public consciousness because herbal products and remedies exist outside their expertise and thus take away from their incomes. The ideal situation would be an East meets West situation that combines current Western medical care with ancient Eastern methods of preventive medicine, which includes a healthier diet, whether it be macrobiotic, vegetarian, or simply lower in salt, a better attitude about one's self and life, and use of the body's natural rhythms and ability to heal itself.

People are not as willing to pay sixty dollars to their doctor as they once were, especially when they have to pay an extra forty dollars for a prescription medicine that often leaves them feeling just as ill as before they began taking it!

That a total balance of the physical, mental, emotional, and spiritual is needed to attain true health, enlightenment, happiness, and love is a truth that's been known since the time of Hippocrates, but over time it has been altered to suit the needs and mentality of current society.

Now it seems people are finally beginning to realize that having expensive clothes and a luxury car doesn't create true happiness. These things may make life a little bit easier and more attractive, but they don't make us better people where it counts—in our hearts. So what do we do?

There have been a lot of well-meaning (and some not-so-well-meaning) books and articles written to show people the way to enlightenment. The idea is that if we are spiritually attuned to inner peace and love and balance in ourselves, our daily stresses will not have as much of a hold on us, and stress will just roll off our backs. But a lot of the material that promises self-love and peace can be confusing. How are we to choose the right book, video, or audiotape to further our path?

Many books and articles state that eight to ten hours of meditation, including approximately two hours of yoga, daily, is the way to reach enlightenment. Yes, that's one way. But it's not the only way. What they usually don't tell you is how to incorporate all that they recommend into the rest of your life.

Not everyone is lucky enough to be able to take a sabbatical from daily commitments and retreat to an ashram or a Zen monastery to practice all of this.

It is not really necessary to go that far to accomplish the same result. Attaining some degree of inner peace is about letting go of our attachments and possessions, relinquishing control of events and people in our lives. To achieve this we need to begin with ourselves at home. It is not our surroundings that will induce the change, but what's inside us. We could go to a monastery and spend our whole life there and yet still not necessarily learn anything.

Daily meditation, yoga, healthier eating, healthier thinking, and proper breathing are all integral to get to where we want to be—where we *need* to be in order to survive. And I believe the intent, or desire, is out there. People want to improve their lives but simply don't know how to incorporate staying centered, being healthy, and having a calm mind into the things they have to do to keep up with the daily onslaught of their very busy schedules and heavy responsibilities.

This book is designed for those of you who want to achieve inner peace and enlightenment in a nine-to-five world (and beyond) without spending time away from family and daily responsibilities. It is divided into three parts: body, mind, and soul. Each chapter discusses a specific technique and gives exercises and/or suggestions that will lead you along the path to inner peace and provide you with a sense of wellness, balance, and control in your life. Most important, the key to these exercises is that they can be done on a daily basis in conjunction with current lifestyles; they are not exclusive to retreats.

Between these two covers, I want to give people the opportunity to explore the myriad ways to attain inner enlightenment and peace and achieve a more manageable and rewarding life. There are a lot of helpful books out there, but none such as this. Most of the other books cover only one subject at a time. This book explores dozens of possibilities you can take advantage of and learn from.

Life is hard enough as it is, and if one person can enrich his life by attaining peace within himself, sharing his love, and getting to the point of doing things for others "just because," with no expectation of return, then we as humans have a chance at survival. Not just monetary survival, but emotional, spiritual, and physical survival.

There is an old adage that says "If even one person attains spiritual enlightenment, the world is enlightened."

That has always sounded great to me. Okay, let's begin.

Part 1

BODY

1

Eating Healthy on a Supermarket Budget

Have you ever tried cooking healthier meals for your family
or friends and gotten the response "Ugh, what is this?"? Your
low-fat or no-fat dinner is left uneaten. You order pizza and
go back to cooking the old way the next night, simply adding
a salad or more vegetables to each meal.

Or have you ever made plans to go to a health-food store
to add quality to your meals—only to discover that the near-
est one is three towns away and is closed by the time you get
off work? And when you finally get there on a Saturday, you
find, to your horror, that organically grown apples are over $2
a pound and a loaf of rice bread costs almost $3. You begin to
wonder whether healthier eating is even within your budget!

It's true that health-food stores are more expensive than
supermarkets, but it's also true that you don't need to shop
exclusively at health-food stores to make healthy meals. As
each day passes, more organically grown food and chemical-
free body products become available in the local supermarket

around the corner. You may still have to go to health-food stores for some specialty items you cannot find elsewhere—things like miso soup, rice bread, seaweed, and rice milk—but that is also changing as the managers of supermarkets have become much more natural-food conscious in recent years. You can now find sprouts in the vegetable aisle and sometimes even a whole section of organically grown fruit and vegetables (although it's usually a small selection). Most modern supermarkets also stock tofu, tahini sauce, bulgur, falafel, miso, seaweed, and whole-wheat flour. Even the mainstream food company Green Giant has gotten into the act with a line of vegetable burgers in all kinds of flavors from plain to Italian to Southwestern and soybean. A neighborhood pizzeria near my home has even begun to list vegetable burgers on their menus alongside all the pizzas, lasagnas, and parmigianas.

The fact that these items are readily available in our supermarkets today makes healthier eating easier than ever. So why do we still shy away from healthy foods? Most people say healthy foods don't taste as good or aren't as filling as the stuff we eat in our day-to-day diet of deli sandwiches and fast-food burgers. But this is just caused by plain unfamiliarity. Some foods may not taste as good as we'd like, but that's because we're not used to their new (or should I say *natural*) flavors, which are actually not so new but are original flavors from before ketchup came along. As a society we have been brainwashed into covering our foods with butter, sour cream, hollandaise sauce—you name it.

How many of us eat corn swathed in butter, or potatoes laden with sour cream, or, the ultimate nosh, french fries with ketchup and salt? If you're used to eating your vegetables swimming in sauce, eating steamed veggies without anything on them may be too severe a switch. Instead, try cutting the amount of whatever you put on top of your vegetables in half and eventually reduce the amount of sauce to nothing.

Your numbed taste buds will eventually come alive to the taste of the vegetables themselves and you'll find that they have a wonderful flavor all their own. No excuses anymore for not eating right!

If you still think that making healthier eating choices is too much of a hassle, next time you eat that hamburger and fries, notice how you feel afterward. Tasted great, right? You feel full, right? Do you also feel lazy, sluggish, kind of sleepy, too? Think there might be a connection between what you ate and how you feel?

How many of you remember the food pyramid guide we got in school that charted the recommended servings of the various food groups we need to eat each day to maintain proper nutrition? I had gotten so used to seeing it and reading about it as I was growing up that I eventually tuned out anything anybody had to say about it. One day, though, I had a realization that made the food pyramid come alive.

I knew all about the "right" amount of salt, fat, and carbohydrates our bodies need to function best, but just because I knew it didn't mean I paid attention to it. I had always eaten pretty much whatever I liked. Consequently, I often felt tired and didn't have any energy. To try and make up for the lack of energy, I drank a lot of coffee. I used to tell people, "I drink eight glasses of water per day, only it's coffee-flavored!" When the caffeine wore off and I came home from work exhausted, I simply went to bed early and repeated the whole process the next day.

For lunch I would bring some leftovers to work or order from fast-food restaurants. One hot summer day a few years ago, about an hour after I finished eating my lunch of reheated pasta from the previous night's dinner, I suddenly felt very droopy and tired and couldn't keep my eyes open. Before I knew it, I fell asleep and then woke up feeling completely drained, instead of refreshed, by the quick (if unexpected) nap. I couldn't understand what had happened. I attributed it to the heat and being overworked, so that night I went to bed early.

This began to happen on a regular basis, and I started to get worried. The pattern was the same each day, and I began to fear I had a medical problem. A few weeks later, with the summer temperature steadily rising, I decided a 98-degree day was too warm for a hot lunch so I ate some cantaloupe and watermelon instead, and, can you believe it? I was awake the whole afternoon! Not only that, I had energy. Wow! What a great feeling! I felt better than I had in a long time.

In my amazement, I wondered what I had done differently that day, and then it occurred to me that there just might be a connection between my unusual energy and my choice of lunch. I decided to experiment. For the next two weeks, I brought various green salads and fruit for lunch and continued to have energy throughout the day. Not only that, I started to feel better emotionally—less bogged down, more aware. I began to feel really good about myself physically and emotionally. As a test, I decided to go back to a heavy, carbohydrate-packed lunch to gauge my reactions, and the old symptoms returned. I promptly felt drained of energy. That was it for me. Right then I made a decision to change my eating habits for good.

My friends, family, and coworkers noticed the change in my lunch menu and were quick to ask whether I was on a diet. I promptly replied "No, just eating healthy." I began to realize that when we eat healthier, there's something that happens that is even more important than the obvious effect of losing weight: we develop a new mental approach to food. Our minds have a tendency to sabotage us by attaching a certain stigma to certain words. *Diet* is a perfect example. It's almost as if your mind is ready to trip you up when you say "diet." But if you say—even to yourself—that you're eating healthier, your mind doesn't know how to sabotage that! Face it, how many people are on diets?

The classic pattern of dieting to lose weight is to start on a diet with fervor and determination, but unless we have an iron will and stick-to-itiveness, we fall off the wagon, so to speak. This is usually followed by a sense of disappointment and disgust. We then binge on foods that we know aren't good for us, but tell ourselves it's okay because we'll start on a *new* diet tomorrow, certain that the new diet will do the trick. Well, guess what? It won't. All that's being done is perpetuating a yo-yo cycle that does nothing for our health—only our waistline. Think of all of the effort and energy that we put into short-term dieting to lose weight (the yo-yoing and constant tiredness and pressure), instead of just making a permanent change in our eating habits, with good health as the goal. All of the energy we'd save would be well worth placing in other areas of our life! A healthy diet should be a way of life, not just a way to get down to the next size in clothes.

Don't get me wrong. I still had my craving for a great thick, deli sandwich or a cheeseburger, and sometimes I allowed myself those things, but the difference I felt after eating something fried or heavy with mayonnaise wasn't worth it. I simply wasn't comfortable. I felt bloated and as if the inside of my body was coated with grease, so I went back to eating simpler, lighter, and healthier food. Eventually I lost the taste for certain foods, and when I tried eating them they didn't sit right in my stomach. It seemed as if I couldn't tolerate anything heavily battered and fried. My body got to the point where it craved foods without heavy sauces and fillers, and I felt quite full after eating a piece of pita bread stuffed with sprouts and beans. Nowadays my idea of an absolutely delicious meal is a bowl of brown rice and beans (kidney beans, aduki beans, or chick peas) with a little oregano and a touch of cayenne pepper, and a salad on the side. Brown and basmatic rices are the most nutritionally balanced of the rices and thereby make a perfect meal—nutritious, delicious and easy to prepare.

Those people who asked me whether I was "still" dieting continued to watch what I ate. You could almost see them waiting for me to "fall." One woman even remarked, "Why are you bothering? You'll only gain the weight back eventually." But weight loss wasn't my goal! Eventually the watching stopped, and I, in turn, began to notice those very people who had commented on my eating were now eating more fruit and lighter lunches than their usual fare of chili dogs and burgers. Some people have even come up to me, thanked me, and said they'd noticed what I'd been eating and my increased energy level, and that they'd begun to eat differently also and felt much better for it. I like to believe I've been able to show others that eating foods that aren't fried or loaded up with fatty, greasy junk doesn't equal dieting—it equals a healthier lifestyle.

Here are a few of my favorite recipes to help you get started. The ingredients can all be found in your supermarket, and your imagination will do the rest. All of these can be doubled or tripled for higher servings.

Sprouts Pita Sandwich

(1 serving)

This is one of my favorites. It's quick, easy and absolutely delicious.

    1 whole-wheat pita
    1 bunch (handful) alfalfa sprouts
    1 can kidney beans (16 ounces)
    Optional: Feta cheese, sliced hard boiled egg, low-fat/
       low-calorie salad dressing or low-fat mayonnaise.

Open the can of kidney beans, rinse and drain well. Tear the top third off of the pita and gently spread open the pocket. Layer the sprouts and beans, beginning with the beans on the bottom. If you're going to put feta cheese in, alternate kidney beans, cheese, sprouts, cheese, and kidney beans.

You can add a boiled egg in any layer. Cut it into slices and slip it into the pocket. If you're using salad dressing, just pour it into the side of the pocket or over the top of the opening. Make sure that, if you're going to travel, you wrap this sandwich tightly in aluminum foil or plastic wrap and carry lots of napkins because it can be quite messy to eat!

Brown Rice and Beans

(2 servings)

This is a quick and nutritious dinner that is guaranteed to fill you up.

1/2 14-ounce box of Success Boil in Bag brown rice or
   one 16-ounce box of brown rice (2 cups)
1 small bag of frozen vegetables, such as peas or lima
   beans
3 cloves of garlic or 1 small onion (*optional*)
2 tablespoons olive oil (*optional*)
1 can kidney beans (16 ounces), rinsed and drained
1 can stewed tomatoes (16 ounces) (*optional*)
1 tablespoon of olive oil

Cook rice according to directions on box. In a separate
pot, boil frozen vegetables (I like to use the whole bag if it's
small. This way, if I don't use all the vegetables with the rice,
I have them for a quick lunch or snack the next day—no
preparation time!). Now, finely chop the garlic and/or onion
and sauté in olive oil until the onions become soft. When
everything is finished cooking, mix together thoroughly in a
large bowl, including the kidney beans.

You can add salt and pepper to taste, but I've found the kidney beans give this dish so much flavor that I don't need any
other spices. You can, however, add some cayenne pepper,
oregano, or any other spices that you like. Hold the mayo!

The list of vegetables that can be added to the basic dish of
brown rice is endless. Try sautéing some chopped carrots or red
and green peppers. Use your imagination!

Ten-Minute Sweet Potato

Another super-quick and nutritious lunch or even a dinner, if
you add a salad, is a sweet potato. Sweet potatoes contain
more vitamins than regular eastern or Idaho potatoes and
they're not as dry.

Wash the potato, cut off both ends and pierce with a fork or a knife. Wrap in plastic wrap and place in a microwave for six minutes on high. When done, turn the potato over and microwave it for another four minutes. Be very careful when you take it out and unwrap it. It is extremely hot and the steam could give you a mild burn. Cut and eat! Use little or no butter. Besides not being needed, it defeats the purpose of eating healthy!

Kidney Burritos

(1 serving)

1 can kidney beans (16 ounces)
5 ounces of low- or no-fat shredded cheese
2 whole-wheat or white-flour tortillas

Rinse the kidney beans. On a tortilla, spread some kidney beans in a single layer. Top with shredded cheese and microwave until the cheese melts. When done, wait a minute or two because it will be very hot, and then fold tortilla in half and eat. This is really good with some salsa for dipping on the side or with some long-grain rice. You can also use corn tortillas, but these tend to break more easily when folded.

Salad Sandwiches

(1 serving)

Salads don't always belong in bowls. Try some leftover salad in a pita pocket or between slices of your favorite bread. It's a great way to get your greens.

Sliced tomatoes
Sliced cucumbers
Mushrooms
Sprouts
2 slices of whole-wheat bread (or your own favorite)
1 teaspoon of low-fat mayonnaise or salad dressing.
Lettuce leaves, torn into small pieces, or leftover salad
Options: Cheese and your imagination

You can toast the bread or not, whatever your preference is, and layer on the lettuce and tomatoes, and the rest of the ingredients (or anything else that strikes your fancy) and enjoy. I like to call this a salad to go! It really is a handy way to eat your salad.

Bean Salad

(1 serving)

1 can of kidney beans (16 ounces), or any beans of your
    choice, drained and rinsed
1/2 red pepper cut into thin strips
Feta cheese to taste.

Mix ingredients and toss well. I found that the beauty of this dish is that it's plenty of food for one for lunch or a light dinner with some accompaniments. And the flavors blend together so wonderfully that no spices are needed, believe it or not! You've got to try this incredibly simple salad to believe it! I threw it together by accident one day as I was mixing together whatever my eye fell on in my fridge in an attempt to make myself something for lunch—and voilà!

NOTE: Be sure you get enough protein in your diet. As you can tell, I'm partial to kidney beans, but any variety of bean will do. Beans are a good substitute for meat products. There are many different kinds of beans in the supermarket, including chick peas, black beans, and lentils. Other beans that are good include aduki, soy, and mung beans, but these are more expensive and probably can be found only in a natural-foods supermarket.

For full protein, combine beans with whole grains such as brown rice, millet, or barley.

For more recipes and tips on healthier eating, refer to the Suggested Reading section at the end of this book.

2

Food Combining

Want to know a great way to stop using Tums and Rolaids? Want to have more energy? Who doesn't? We get our energy from food—the breakdown of the food in our digestive system, to be exact. Our stomachs use particular digestive juices to break down particular kinds of food. If we eat something that cannot be broken down and used efficiently by our cells, it becomes fermented and putrefied in our stomachs, thus generating toxins in our body. Toxins equal heartburn!

Acid is necessary in your stomach to properly break down and digest foods, but our bodies are not capable of digesting more than one kind of food at a time. Confused? Let me explain: You eat a steak (protein) for dinner. To properly break this food down and use its nutrients, you need a particular type of acid-based digestive juice. Clear? Along with your steak, you have a baked potato (although potatoes are vegetables, once they are baked and have lost their water they become pure starch). Your stomach needs another kind of digestive juice to break down the potato, an alkaline-based juice. Now you have alkaline and acid in your stomach at the same time, and (you may remember from chemistry class) they neutralize each other, so your food takes longer to be digested.

Since your stomach is not digesting the food (because its digestive juices are neutralized), your body recognizes the need for breakdown and produces more acid, which is again neutralized. Remember, this is taking time and energy, and it keeps happening until, eventually, the food, which is never properly digested, is finally moved into the intestines and you are left with heartburn, possible food allergies, and a host of other disturbances. The first third of our digestive process takes place in our saliva as we chew our food. The other two thirds of digestion occurs in our stomach and small intestine. So, in essence, indigestion begins with not chewing enough in the first place to properly begin to break down the food. Each bite of a meal should be chewed at least fifteen to twenty times.

The real reason you should be eating is for energy, not simply because food tastes good. To get the most energy from your meals you need to learn to combine your food properly. The wrong food combinations can undermine digestion, absorption, and elimination cycles by causing food to ferment in your stomach, creating heartburn and intestinal gas (flatulence). Foods eaten in correct combinations, however, will pass quickly through the entire digestive system, making a smooth flow of the digestive process, which can help you lose weight, relieve stomach upset, and help you get the most nutrients out of the food you've eaten.

Proper food combining is quite simple. Proteins should be eaten with vegetables, and starches are also good with vegetables (actually, anything is good with vegetables!), but protein and starches shouldn't be eaten together. It would be better to eat complex carbohydrates at one meal, protein at another meal, and save the fruits for snacks. If you combine your foods improperly, you will need much more energy to properly digest the various structures of food, leaving you feeling sluggish and tired. Animal proteins alone can take up to six hours to digest. Imagine the havoc wreaked upon your digestive tract as the refined sugars from your dessert sit in your stomach fermenting while waiting for the stomach to finish digesting the steak you had as a main course. Ugh!

It is also important not to eat fruit with or right after a meal. It will only ferment what's already in your stomach. You should eat fruit twenty minutes before a meal, but not right after. Fruit needs little energy to assimilate and goes from your stomach into your intestines within twenty minutes. Therefore, by waiting twenty minutes before you eat anything else, there will be no residue of the fruit in your stomach to cause digestive problems. If you really need that peach cobbler or apple pie for dessert, wait at least 45 minutes after your last bite of dinner to allow your stomach to settle down.

Eating the proper combinations of foods can give you added energy, assists in weight loss, and keep your intestines cleaner.

What I have offered here is a very basic, general outline of food combining. To truly grasp the impact combining has on the wear and tear of our digestive tract and our energy levels, one must be fully familiarized with starches, sugars (complex, simple, refined), carbohydrates (complex), cellular structure of food, and the proper way to prepare food to release the proper enzymes. It has all the makings of a science.

The Egg Project by nutritionist Gary Null offers an in-depth look at a guide to proper eating. (See the Suggested Reading section for details.)

3

Acupressure: Hitting the Spot

In 1913, Dr. William Fitzgerald, an American physician, published *Zone Therapy*, a book in which he described the human body as having ten longitudinal zones, five on each side of the body, from the top of the head through the toes and fingers. Within these zones he located pinpoint areas that were painful to the touch. By applying pressure to certain points of the fingers and hands, Dr. Fitzgerald felt one could relieve pain in other parts of the body in the same zone.

In the 1930s, Eunice Ingham, an American physical therapist, combined her knowledge of Chinese healing techniques, which called for applying pressure and massaging certain areas of the body, with Dr. Fitzgerald's work on body zones to develop a bodywork technique that focused the body's energy for healing purposes. In applying the bodywork technique in her work with patients, Ingham discovered that the feet provided a greater response than the hands did in overall improved body functioning, and she gradually mapped zones and pressure pinpoint areas of the entire body through the feet. Before her death in 1974, her hard work and enthusiasm paid off as reflexology, as her work came to be called, became recognized as a science.

Zone therapy, foot massage, reflexology, and acupressure all operate on the same principle as acupuncture, the ancient Chinese therapy that is based on the belief that disease is the result of an imbalance of energy. In acupuncture specific points in the body are stimulated with needles so that the blocked energy is released and dispersed.

Instead of using needles, acupressure uses finger-pressing techniques to break through energy blocks and calcium deposits that, under stressful situations, pool in the muscles under the skin's surface, and in the muscle tissue. Finger pressure is a simple, safe, and extremely effective way of relaxing and relieving these blocks.

Today, reflexologists work primarily with the feet (and sometimes hands and other points—meridians—throughout the body) by applying steady, deep, thumb or forefinger pressure that covers most of the foot and part of the ankle. By locating a tender spot on the foot, the reflexologist can determine which section of the body it refers to. Generally, the intensity of the pain is related to the magnitude of the problem elsewhere in the body and its duration. When improvement in the body's functions occurs, the original sore point on the foot is no longer so painful.

Reflexology works wonders on the feet, and you can either practice it on yourself or work on someone else. It can be done at home or in the office. A quick ten-minute foot massage will revitalize your energy level and give you a physical check-in to see what areas of your body, if any, are not as productive as they should be. The foot chart located in this chapter is intended as a reference for the various points on your feet and the organs they correspond to.

Let the Fingers Do the Walking!

When working on your own feet, sit in a comfortable position with the foot you're tending resting on your opposite knee. If you're working on another person's feet, he can relax comfortably in a chair, couch, or on the floor, with his feet straight out in front of him. Make sure that you are both comfortable. Hold the foot with one hand and use the thumb or forefinger of the other hand to apply steady pressure in a circular motion. You can use some talcum powder to absorb any moisture on the hands or feet. Start by applying pressure to the top, sides, front, and bottom of the big toe. Work down the inside of the foot all the way to the heel.

Give a general massage to the entire foot, "kneading" it with your thumbs and fingers, and note any sore spots. If a pain is felt in any area, you know that the corresponding area of the body is not functioning properly and should be looked into. (See chart for corresponding areas.)

Watch the face of the person whose foot you're working on for signs of extreme pain or discomfort. Reduce the pressure if there is too much pain, but pay attention to the painful areas and after working on both feet, go back to the sore spots and briefly work on them again, to help loosen any muscle knots. If a spot is still too painful, massage the surrounding area. Always remember to go gently. Overmanipulation of these sore spots can be counterproductive and do more harm than good. If anything, work on those areas on the next massage. Return to the toes and work down the rest of the foot toward the heel. Next, work on the back of the heel, and the sides of the ankle, followed by the top of the foot, all the while being aware of any sore spots. You can end the massage by gently kneading and rubbing the entire foot and ankle area.

Reflexology Chart

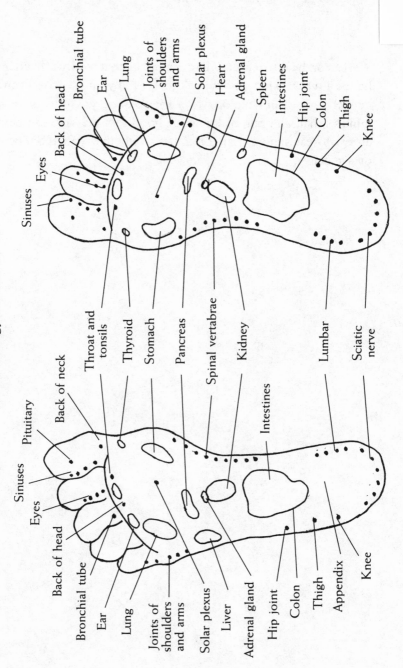

NOTE: For health reasons, I recommend that you wash your hands after working on anyone's feet, even your own. You can give the gift of reflexology to a friend or to yourself for ten minutes, half an hour, or longer. A good foot massage can put an ear-to-ear smile on anyone's face—whether you're a giver or a receiver.

4

Common Scents About Aromatherapy

How many times have you smelled the aroma of something baking, such as homemade bread, and found yourself immersed in memories of your mother's or grandmother's kitchen when you were a child? The sense of smell has a very strong connection to the emotions. Often, a particular scent can produce a rush of emotions that envelop you before your mind can replay the scenes attached to those emotions.

Aromatherapy is the practice of using scents and essential oils for relaxation, healing, worship, and attracting love. It can employ perfumes, incense, oils, wood, or lotions. The history of aromatherapy dates back to the Romans, Greeks, Egyptians, and before. Aromas are a powerful stimulus to heightening spirituality, sharpening psychic awareness, stimulating memories of the past (good and bad), and promoting restful sleep.

Aromatherapy has always been around as perfume, but it has been reborn in recent years as a real therapy in mainstream society. Using original, raw ingredients of scent and methods of applying this scent, aromatherapy is an alternative healing practice for those who want to go beyond the traditional methods of dealing with illness, in which profit margins often dictate that we treat symptoms rather than the core cause of the diseases. Conventional aromatherapy (essential oils used to heal the body and psyche) is increasing in popularity. Some scents are used to increase physical energy and mental alertness while others are used to reduce the effects of stress.

The Past

We have all heard the story of those three wise men who traveled far and followed a star, to bring gifts of frankincense and myrrh to the newborn Jesus. Frankincense and myrrh are more than just a part of the Nativity story. The aroma of frankincense has been used in spiritual practices for more than three thousand years to help reduce physical stress and heighten spiritual awareness, while myrrh, also used in many different spiritual practices, dates back even further, to four thousand years, and has also been used to awaken spiritual awareness.

Because both of these resins have a history of use for spiritual awareness, and were present at the time of Jesus' birth, I like to think that this may explain some of the biblical stories of Jesus' spiritual awareness throughout his youth and short life. Frankincense and myrrh may have played a unique part in his spiritual growth. Can you imagine if these resins had been lit in the hospital rooms when our mothers had been giving birth to us? I can't help but wonder if it would have made a difference in the way we think, feel, and perceive each other and our maker.

Scents from flowers and herbs were used for more than just spiritual awakening, though that was a significant part of their role. The Egyptians used aromatic plant essences as tributes to certain deities and essences in temples as offerings to the gods and goddesses. One such incense, called kyphi, was used during religious festivals and was also eaten for its medicinal effects. Essential oils were used in ancient Egyptian culture to anoint the bodies of the dead. Sealed jars of perfume have also been found in many Egyptian tombs, presumably for use in the afterlife.

The Greeks also had an interesting history with aromatherapy. They believed that the fresh scents rising from living plants maintained physical health. It was because of this belief that laurel (bay) leaves came to be used as a crown in Olympic victories. The aroma of the leaves from the crown would ensure physical stamina during the rest of the games and led to victory. The Greeks also had houses designed so that rooms opened up into flower and herb gardens.

The Greeks also understood the importance of inhaling certain aromas to ease physical ailments. Oils scented with quince or white violet were used to ease stomach upset, grape-leaf perfume was used to clear the head, and garlands of roses were used to relieve headaches. When the Romans conquered the Greeks, they carried the use of scents one step further by soaking their cups and bowls with aromatic oils prior to using them.

The ancient Hawaiians had their own uses for plant essences. They used wild ginger juice in massage and coconut oil to scent their bedding and clothing as well as to anoint their hair and bodies to help maintain moisture and prevent dryness caused by hours of sun and ocean swimming.

Clearly, in one form or another, aromatherapy has been with us from earliest times. People have used the powers of fragrant plants to produce specific changes in their lives. These changes included spiritual connection with deities, attracting a mate, heightening sexual arousal, purifying the body prior to ritual, healing the sick, and guarding against negative energies.

The Present

Today the use of essential oils is the primary way aromatherapy is practiced. You've heard of them, you've probably seen them in New Age stores, and even in stalls and stores in malls, but what exactly are essential oils? An essential oil is the aromatic substance that occurs naturally in plants. It is what gives roses and garlic their particular scents. Bottled essential oils are the distilled products of naturally aromatic plant materials (such as leaves or petals). To confuse things even further, let's say you pick up a bottle whose label reads "oil of jasmine." That doesn't mean it's an *essential oil*, but rather that it's a fragrance that's been produced in a laboratory by mixing appropriate chemicals to reproduce the scent of jasmine. It is *not* the essential oil of jasmine. Many distributors sell synthetic oils in the United States under the guise of essential oils because they are cheap and easy to make. Synthetics make up the bulk of what we see in the stores. These are fine for their aromatic properties, but to use the synthetic oils for their physical healing properties won't work because they are not refined from the true parts of the flower or plant.

The beauty and wonder of *true* essential oils is that they are from plants, and these plants have a direct link with the

Earth. The energy of the sun, the nutrients of the soil, and the soothing and quenching element of the rain resonate in the essence of the oil. They have all worked together to create nature. We, too, as humans, are of the Earth and resonate with the same vibrations, so when using true essential oils, a link is made vibrationally and spiritually between our own energy and the condensed energy of the plant. The merging of the two energies is what enables the changes in our physical body and our psyche to take place.

The use of aromatherapy in physical healing is more common in Europe than in the United States. Studies at hospitals in France have supported the use of aroma in healing, but we have yet to find support for it here. In the United States, the antiseptic smell of doctors' offices and hospitals carries negative connotations of illness and death. Imagine what it would be like if the next time you were sitting in your doctor's office or laid up in a hospital room, you could smell wildflowers or sandalwood instead of stale air bearing everybody else's germs in it? I wonder how much the rate of healing would increase?

In the 1930s, an English doctor named Edward Bach believed that if a patient's emotional imbalance was corrected, the body's natural defenses in throwing off illness would be strengthened. The essences are not to be used for specific *physical* ailments, but for states of mind and mood. He extracted oils from thirty-eight flowers of nonpoisonous plants, bushes, and trees and tested them for their effect on mood. The result of his work is known as Bach Flower Therapy. Each essence is used to treat a specific mental or emotional state.

In general, Bach Flower Essences are available in liquid, and used in doses of four drops, three times a day—morning, noon, and evening—and are taken on an empty stomach. They can be used internally or externally. Treatment should be continued for six or seven weeks, or until improvement is shown. Bach Flower Essences are now also available as creams, that can be used internally or externally.

These flower essences are not harmful or habit-forming and have no known side effects. They have been useful in altering such moods as fear, worry, anger, and depression—all of which can cause illness or inhibit normal healing. The essences work on the emotional side of the sick person and help to transform the negative attitudes into positive ones. A positive attitude allows the body to better fight disease physically and eases emotional stress. Bach Flower Essences can be purchased in many New Age stores and health-food stores, and there are a number of books and pamphlets available that discuss in detail which essence is best for which person. Some pamphlets will even provide a quiz to help you determine the proper essence for you.

Perfume companies have known for years that natural scents affect our psyches. In Europe aromatherapy is used primarily for physical healing, while in the United States, the focus is on emotional healing. The perfume industry is based on a "feel good" dynamic: they take the oils and extracts from live plants (flowers and fruits), chemically copy them (to help reduce the cost of using live materials), and then mix them with an oil extract from animal glands to produce a scent that is so "intoxicating" you'll not only feel more confident about yourself, but no one will be able to resist your charms.

Fresh Flowers

Whether you buy fresh-cut flowers or pick them yourself, always treat flowers and plants with respect. They are a part of the Earth, and when you look at them in your vase or in a field they should be a reminder of the magnificence of nature. Plants possess the same type of energy that's in our bodies. Studies have shown that talking to and even playing music for plants will enhance their growth more than simply watering them every day and walking away. Plants sense the energy that comes from us and revel in the vibration we give off, much as children revel and grow when their parents shower them with love and attention rather than merely feeding them and taking them to and from school and childhood activities.

Flowers and plants can be thought of as our children in a sense. Always place flowers in fresh water. For optimum freshness, and to keep flowers from wilting, a quarter of an inch should be cut from the bottoms of the stems immediately before placing them in the water, so as to enhance the flow of water up into the stems and leaves. As soon as a flower is cut, a resin forms around the cut area and seals it, inhibiting a full flow of water.

Heavily fragrant flowers are best cut just before sunrise when their essential-oil content is at its peak. However, some flowers, such as jasmine, give off higher amounts of perfume at night, so you might want to collect them then.

Change the water frequently and, if you want the continual aroma, replace waning flowers with fresh ones.

Leaves

The leaves of some plants and herbs, such as basil and rosemary, are best collected in a fresh state. Some fruit and vegetable markets sell clumps of fresh herbs in standing water, which helps ensure their freshness. Treat the leaves the same way as the fresh flowers described previously, and keep in fresh water. A simple bowl will do fine. Replace as the leaves wane.

Dried Flowers, Seeds, and Wood

Using any of these three requires a little more preparation than just putting them in a bowl. To release the most scent of spices and seeds such as cloves and cinnamon, lightly crush them using a mortar and pestle or between two rocks.

For dried leaves and flowers, gently crush them using your hands to break them up, but it is important to wash your hands before you do this to remove any of your body's natural oils that can mingle with and contaminate the true essence of the flowers.

Woods such as sandalwood and cedar usually have enough of an aromatic scent as whole pieces, but sometimes they need a little help. If you find that the aroma is not strong enough, rub the wood on a grater for some shavings. Those few seconds of grating will be enough to release more of the scent.

Essential Oils

Using true essential oils can be costly, so do so sparingly. You might want to try fabricated bottled essences. Place two to three drops on a cotton ball and inhale. If you don't have cotton balls, a fresh handkerchief can be used, but make sure it was not washed in heavily scented detergent! This will thwart your purpose because you'll be smelling jasmine and Tide. Not a good combo, believe me!

A good tip is to hand-wash a handkerchief in unscented soap and place a few drops of the oil on a portion of it and hold it up to your nose. Here are a few other ways to use oils:

Potpourri Simmers

These pretty ceramic bowls are available everywhere from major department stores like Kmart to small specialty stores and boutiques. A small bowl, called a simmering pot, is filled with drops of oil, dried scented flowers (potpourri), or perfumed wax pellets and water. Its lid, which has holes in it to allow the fragrance to waft through your house, is placed on top. The whole thing sits on top of a smaller ceramic holder, where a tea candle is placed and lit, thus letting the heat from the flame gently warm the material inside the pot to a temperature that does not boil the water or oils but heats it enough to release the essences.

Electric potpourri simmers are also available. With no need for tea candles, these may be more convenient for some people. This is a great way to release the aroma throughout your home but you must keep an eye on simmers when using oil or water to make sure it doesn't evaporate and leave you with a container hot to the touch and melted flower petals! Perfumed waxed pellets or dried flowers in water are used with potpourri simmers as an alternative to using oils.

Potpourri Rings

These are metal rings that you place on top of your light bulbs. They have a groove inside the ring where you can pour in the essential oil. Place the ring on top of the light bulb in a lamp that is on in whatever room you'll be spending time in. The heat from the light bulb warms the oil and releases the scent throughout the room in a very gentle manner. It works really well.

Baths

This can become a tricky area because not all oils can be used directly on the skin. Some citrus oils (orange, lemon grass, lemon balm) and strong spices (clove, cinnamon, nutmeg) are highly irritating to the mucous membranes and to skin in general, resulting in burning and itching. Always read about the oil's properties on the label and make sure it's safe to use directly on the skin, or ask a knowledgeable person about toxicity to the skin before buying an essential oil you plan to use in baths. There are many books on oils and their properties that can serve as reference guides; they can be found in the health section of your local bookstore. I want to make it clear that the oils I'm talking about here do not include oils specially formulated and touted for baths and showers. The focus of my warnings is on *true* essential oils that are not diluted or reproduced chemically in any way.

Once you choose an oil, add six to ten drops, one drop at a time, to warm water for an aromatic, relaxing bath. One drop at a time or gently and slowly pouring the oil is recommended to ensure that the oil does not evaporate rapidly from the bath water's heat. Again, please check the oil's properties to prevent any possible skin problems.

I cannot stress enough that the only real danger in aromatherapy is in the use of essential oils. Remember, essential oils are a highly concentrated form of plants, and though some herbs can be ingested in cooking or used as incense, direct contact with the oil the herb contains can cause irritation.

Sage is a good example. It is a commonly used herb in cooking, but it contains a toxic substance called thujone that is harmful if used as an essential oil. Mugwort, fennel, marjoram, penny royal, and some other essential oils have also been determined to be dangerous. Pregnant women, especially, need to be careful with essential oils.

Some important points to remember:

- If you choose to use essential oils for aromatherapy treatment, it is imperative that you know at least a little bit of the oil's background, since certain oils have been determined to be hazardous and should be avoided altogether or used only with caution. Above all, *no essential oils should be taken internally,* pregnant or not!
- Some oils may cause an allergic reaction in some people but not in others, so use all new oils with caution, a little bit at a time, until you're sure that you will not have an allergic reaction.
- Essential oils should *always* be diluted with another oil such as hazelnut, sesame, or sunflower when applied directly to the skin.
- If you discover you have an allergic reaction to a scent, stop using it immediately.
- When in doubt about using a particular scent, use the fresh or dried plant instead of the essential oil.

Some Essential Oils With Known Allergic Reactions

Basil: Should *not* be taken internally in the form of an oil.
Bergamot: If the skin has been anointed with this oil and then exposed to the sun, severe sunburn can result.
Camphor: Prolonged inhalation causes headache.
Cinnamon Bark and Leaf: Skin irritants. Do not anoint with these or use in baths. Cinnamon bark *can* be ingested and works immediately in raising blood sugar.

Clary Sage: Do not use with alcohol. Prolonged inhalation may cause headache.

Clove Bud, Stem, and Leaf: Skin irritant. Do not anoint with these or use in bath.

Fennel, Bitter: Irritant. Can cause epileptic attacks. Not to be used by pregnant women.

Frankincense: May irritate skin.

Hyssop: Can cause epileptic attacks, possibly other problems. Do not use if pregnant.

Lemon: Irritant. Do not anoint with this or use in baths.

Lemon Balm: Irritant. Do not anoint with this or use in baths.

Lemon Grass: Irritant. Do not anoint with this or use in baths.

Lemon Verbena: Irritant. Do not anoint with this or use in baths.

Marjoram: Not for use by pregnant women.

Mugwort: Essential oil is hazardous and should not be used.

Myrrh: May cause skin irritation if anointed with or used in baths. Do not use during pregnancy.

Oregano: Irritant. Do not anoint with this or use in baths.

Penny royal: Very toxic. Do not use. Pregnant women especially should avoid this essential oil.

Peppermint: Skin irritant. Do not anoint with this or use in baths.

Rue: Dangerous! Do not use in any way.

Sage (Dalmatian): Toxic, can cause epileptic attacks. Not to be used by those who have high blood pressure.

Thyme: A hazardous, toxic essential oil. Skin irritant. Should not be used in essential oil form at all.

Ylang-Lang: Prolonged inhalation may cause headache.

Essential oils, if used intelligently, can be a pleasant way for us to heal or create change in our lives while enjoying nature's bounty of beautiful fragrances.

Incense

Ah, my favorite! It seems almost anywhere you go these days you'll find incense (also called perfume sticks) being sold, from specialty shops to local pharmacies. Incense comes in cones, sticks, or in loose granules. The cones and sticks are lit, and the flame is left until the tip of the stick glows red as you gently blow on it. Then the flame is blown out. Incense granules are placed on a charcoal tablet in a dish and lit. Personally, I think incense is one of the easiest and cheapest ways to experience the full effect of aromatherapy. Essential oils can be expensive, but if used sparingly and with care, can last a long time. Fresh flowers are relatively inexpensive, especially if you pick them yourself, but if you're getting into the more fragrant flowers, they can also become quite an expense. Incense sticks and cones, on the other hand, can be bought almost anywhere for a minimal cost—usually $1.00 for ten sticks! The granules run a few dollars more.

A stick or cone of incense can burn for fifteen to twenty minutes, but the aroma lingers for a long time afterward. Just about every scent in nature can be found in incense, along with many wonderful and exotic combinations.

There is one very special shop near my home where incense is lit every day and the wonderful aroma hugs everything in the store. When I get home I take what I've bought out of the bag, and the smell of the incense lingers on for hours! Another great idea is to take your favorite incense sticks and use them as book markers.

Aromatherapy is a highly personal method of healing. Every flower, seed, wood, herb, and leaf that has been written about has certain sensory and physical healing properties attributed to it, but keep in mind that they may not affect everyone in the same way. Our sense of smell is highly personal and has a very strong tie to our memories, both conscious and unconscious.

What one person may find relaxing, another may find emotionally irritating. Experiment with different aromas. Many places that sell oils have sample bottles that you can open and smell. But don't just smell them from the bottle. Place a few drops on the inside of your wrist so it can mix with the oils of your body and give you a truer sense of the smell of the oil and how it affects you physically and emotionally. Try them and notice their effects on you—emotional and physical. Are the effects pleasing? Do they bring up any particular feelings or memories? Do you feel peaceful? Does your heart suddenly start to race? Do they make you sick to your stomach? Do they remind you of old gym sneakers or of the Earth after a rainstorm?

Above all, don't force yourself to use a scent just because you want to attain a level of something that is supposed to be characteristic of a particular scent. For example, a book says that the scent of wood aloe promotes love and spirituality, but when you smell it, it reminds you of a locker room. That particular scent would be useless in evoking those responses in you and a waste of your money. Don't choose scents based solely on how a book or some other person tells you you should feel. Rather, choose scents that appeal to you on some personal level. Experiment, be open, and above all have fun!

5

Yoga: The Spiritual Side

Yoga is an ancient Eastern Indian belief system designed for the improvement of body, mind, and spirit. The word *yoga* derives from a Sanskrit term meaning "to join." To join what? To join or connnect the body and mind in an effort to return the self to its original state of perfect being—the ultimate goal of being one with God and the universe. When we are one—"joined"—and have reached this state of perfect relaxation in our minds and bodies, we have attained perfect enlightenment and are at peace with everything inside and outside of us.

Yoga can be a very fulfilling experience. The physical aspect of yoga—postures and breathing—are practiced to reduce anxiety, stretch the muscles, and allow proper flow of energy (chi), oxgyen, and blood through the body. The mental aspects of yoga—meditation and mantras—are intended to help focus the mental and emotional state of the practitioner. This physical and mental combination work together to provide the opportunity to attain a perfect state of being.

Breathing is another very important element in yoga. Yogic breathing revitalizes the body and leaves the mind feeling calmer. Daily practice of yoga postures and breathing techniques increases clarity, mental awareness, and concentration. Yoga practice doesn't end there. It also includes disciplines in diet, breath control, and concentration. So there is more to yoga than contortionlike maneuvers. There's a whole system of beliefs that support various postures.

The postures, or asanas, are meant to open up the body's various joints, relieving pressure on the cartilage and readjusting bone positions to restore proper alignment. After a yoga practice you will often feel more energized and alert because by restoring alignment and freeing any blockages, you have allowed oxygen to flow more freely to the body's tissues and brain. There are many books and magazines dedicated to the yoga enthusiast, but how do you know which yoga would be good for you?

There are various kinds of yoga disciplines, but despite the differences, the core meaning is the same—increasing the peacefulness of your mind and reducing tension. For the purpose of this chapter, we will be mainly concerned with postures practiced in Hatha yoga.

As a discipline, yoga should be enjoyed one step at a time and not undertaken with trepidation because you can barely touch your toes let alone place one foot directly behind your head. The joy in attaining anything is in the journey.

Yoga has entered the mainstream and has become more accepted by the general public in recent years. Whether that's due to a new open-mindedness today or just to a desire to seek gentler exercise, no one's sure. But with the help of the increasing popularity of magazines such as *Yoga*

Journal, information about this Eastern practice is reaching beyond a select audience to the general public. Yoga is becoming the preferred alternative to working out at the gym as a way to tone the body and achieve flexibility. An additional benefit is that yoga also helps the practitioner attain an inner calmness.

This ancient art has been practiced for thousands of years, but until recently has been held in low regard in our Western culture. I remember watching Lilas Falan twenty years ago on a local public TV station doing postures I thought were impossible for the human body to achieve. She was the alternative to Jack LaLanne's morning jumping jacks. Today she is still doing her postures on her syndicated television show and looking much the same as she did twenty years ago. She has also released a series of Yoga videos recently. With tapes by Ali Magraw, Jane Fonda and Raquel Welch available, videos for yoga have also increased in popularity.

Hatha Yoga

Hatha Yoga is practiced through the control of breathing exercises and physical postures, and the focus is held for a particular length of time. Its primary goal is to gain control of attentiveness and achieve relaxation. Through Hatha Yoga we learn detachment from the body, thus enabling the spirit to become the leader of the body instead of its servant. Breathing exercises, in particular, are practiced rigorously. Practitioners of this yoga believe that attaining oneness is a state of mind, and one way to do that is by keeping attention fixed to the present.

Raja Yoga

It is important to be familiar with and master Hatha Yoga before going on to Raja Yoga. The goal of Raja Yoga is to develop character and strength. It is geared more for the mind than Hatha yoga is, in that it stresses complete stillness of the mind and becoming master over it. If you don't have the control of the physical body that is gained by practicing Hatha Yoga, you run the risk of "burn out" from the energies that are created in Raja Yoga.

Raja Yoga, also called Astanga Yoga, involves following eight steps, also called the "eightfold path."

1. *Abstention (yama):* Abstaining from having or thinking about evil intentions.
2. *Devotion (niyama):* Having good intentions.
3. *Posture (asana):* Body positions used to quiet the body down.
4. *Breathing (pranayama):* Controlled or energized breathing.
5. *Retraction of the senses (pratyahara):* Eliminating all sensory awareness of objects surrounding you.
6. *Fixation of attention (dharana):* Steadying the mind by focusing it on one object—first real and then imaginary.
7. *Fusive apprehension (dhyana):* The state of mind of intuitiveness.
8. *Fully integrated consciousness (samadhi):* The disappearance of your awareness of self. Becoming one with the universe.

Tantra Yoga

This is probably the most difficult and complex of all the yogas. This is a very detailed yoga, and the information I'm offering here is merely scratching the surface to give you an idea of what various yogas encompass. Tantra includes the teachings and self-discipline of all the other yogas, but achieving the state of pure bliss and loss of self-awareness is the goal. The way to reach that goal is by disconnecting from the body by abstaining from sex. This is a rare yoga in that its teachings about how to achieve this state of bliss are more secret than those of other, more popular, yogas.

Integral Yoga

This is probably the most popular yoga practiced in the United States aside from Hatha Yoga. Its goal is to combine aspects from the various branches of yoga and integrate them into a yoga that will help develop every aspect of the self using the mind, body, intellect, will, and heart, and using service to others, postures, mantras, meditations, and breathing.

Karma Yoga

Karma is a universal principal that every good deed, action, or thought sows the seed for another good deed, and every bad deed, action, or thought gets reciprocated as a negative to the sender or doer. It's the spiritual version of every action has an equal and opposite reaction. The results of these actions can be an immediate result or something that won't come to fruition until sometime in the future or, as some believe, in the next life. Instead of postures or breathing exercises, this yoga is practiced in everyday living through work and service to others and ourselves, and therefore is recognized as the yoga of *action*. The goal of this yoga is to achieve selflessness in our actions and our very being.

Bhakti Yoga

Bhakti Yoga is known as the yoga of devotion. It's when we devote our entire being—mind, body, action, thoughts—to a deity, profession, person, or country, for example, and we become one with our devotion. When we become one with something—wholeheartedly support it, and believe in it, we have a feeling of unity with the commitment. This devotion ties in with the good karma and sets us on the yogic path of devotion.

The benefits of yoga are greatly enhanced when practiced in conjunction with a healthy diet (see chapter 1) and stretching exercises (see chapter 7). When practicing yoga and stretching, it's best to wear loose, unrestrictive clothing and do the postures on an empty stomach, with a rolled up blanket or mat on the floor for certain postures. If you do not want to practice these postures alone or feel you may not be doing them correctly, you can join a yoga group. Look in your phone book under yoga, or go to your local health-food store and ask the employees if they know of any group or individual instructor. Usually people offering their holistic services will have fliers in health-food stores or in New Age bookstores.

If you go to a yoga institute or some other place where yoga classes are held, or as you flip through yoga magazines, you may see structures that are called props. These are intended to help you reach a certain position that you wouldn't be able to get into on your own—at least in the beginning.

The first time I saw a prop, I had no idea what it was, but I decided to give it a try, thinking all the while that I was going to get rope burn or feel foolish hanging like a bat, but I was quite surprised by my flexibility. The prop I'm thinking of in particular is a rack with loops of rope hanging from it that I saw at a spiritual center. I was able to put my forearms on the floor, and still be quite comfortable. Afterward I was truly shocked at the amount of energy and vitality I felt coursing through my body. I felt as though I had just spent ten minutes jumping rope. It was absolutely refreshing!

When I inquired about other props around the room (to me, some looked like giant, warped snow shoes), I learned that props help a person attain the full movement and position of a yoga posture without having to worry about holding a position, which can be awkward at first. Thus the mind is free to concentrate. People can get the full effect of what a yoga position is supposed to feel like—the true coursing of energy—without having to worry about balance.

When I mentioned the idea of props to a friend who is a veteran of yoga, he told me he felt it was cheating to use props because the purpose of yoga is to discipline your body and mind, and when you use props, you're not fully disciplining yourself. You're doing Americanized yoga. Personally, I think using props is helpful for beginners, so they'll know what it's like to be in certain positions. I do believe, however, that once body and mind are strong enough, props should be discarded.

How to Do It

To get you on the yellow brick road of health and peaceful-ness, I have included illustrations of body postures (asanas) you would do in a beginner Hatha Yoga class. Besides pos-tures, beginner-level Hatha Yoga will teach breathing tech-niques (*pranayama*) and cleansing practices (*kriyas*).

Listed below each illustration are the benefits of the pos-ture so you'll know *why* you're trying to see your backside, besides knowing that the twist is *good* for you!

These postures should be done with care. As with any physical exercise you do, do not overexert your muscles. Bend or twist to *flex* and *stretch* your body. Yoga is a gentle discipline, and the perfect posture should be achieved grad-ually, especially if you've never practiced yoga before, or have had only minimal physical exercise. If you push too hard or too quickly, you can cause serious damage to your muscles. When working with children, particular care should be taken not to overexert them. Gentle but constant stretching is the best approach. Another important word of caution: If you are pregnant, consult a doctor or yoga ther-apist. Hatha Yoga can be practiced by people of any age, whether you're thin, fat, fit, flabby, stiff, or flexible, but even so, care must be taken.

Since Hatha Yoga is a mental as well as a physical disci-pline, it is beneficial to begin with a chant or prayer. Sit in a comfortable position with your back straight. Many people choose to sit in the classic Lotus position, with legs crossed and each ankle resting comfortably on top of the opposite leg. Take a few deep breaths and focus your mind. Begin a chant or repeat a word or phrase that has a meaning for you (such as a mantra) and concentrate on that word. *Om* is a popular choice. (for others, see chapter 10 on mantras and affirmations.)

Before going into the full-body poses, begin with the following eye exercises. These exercises relax the eye muscles, increase circulation, tone the optic nerves, and are a general aid in improving eyesight. They are intended to help the eyes focus better. You may feel a little nauseated at first, but do as much as you can. It's important to rest your eyes after each set of these exercises by closing your eyes and sitting quietly for a minute or two. Repeat each exercise ten to fifteen times.

- *Vertical* Move your eyes up and down as far as possible.
- *Horizontal* Move your eyes horizontally, from left to right.
- *Diagonal* Move your eyes from the upper right corner to the lower left corner.
- *Half Circles* Move your eyes in a half-circle from lower right corner to the lower left. Then switch to the lower half of the circle. Start at the upper right, look down, and up to the lower left.
- *Full Circles* Move the eyes in a full circle.

Sun Salutation: This is really one pose but has twelve steps. If you do each of the steps quickly, they will energize you, but if you do them slowly and methodically, they will relax your mind and body. The Sun Salutation also increases circulation throughout the entire body. Repeat the entire sequence three to four times. You can increase repetitions when you feel comfortable doing so. Hold each pose for ten to fifteen seconds.

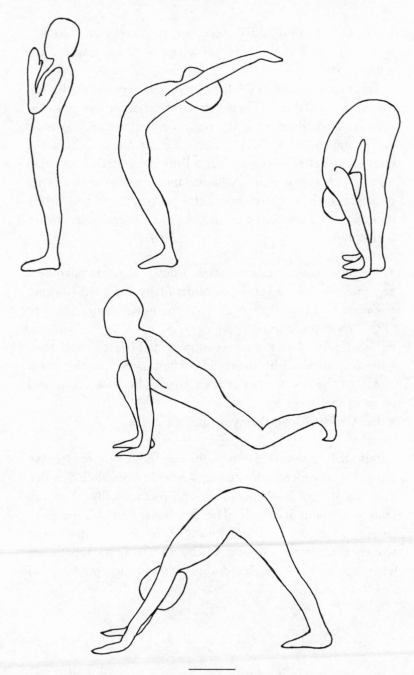

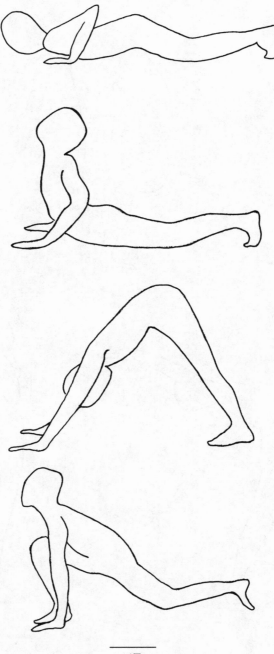

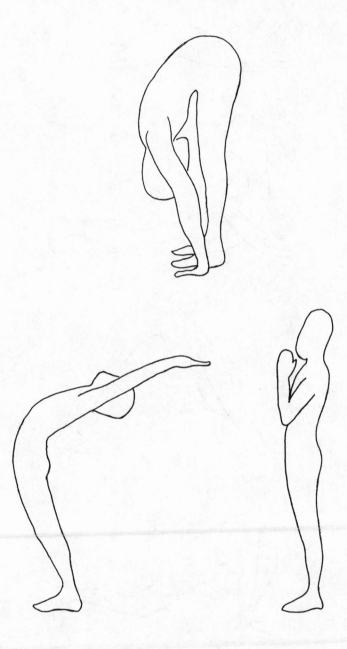

Cobra: The Cobra pose exercises the back muscles, spine, and cranial nerves; expands the chest; and relieves backache. In women, it helps tone the reproductive organs. Hold pose for ten to fifteen seconds and repeat twice, concentrating between the shoulder blades.

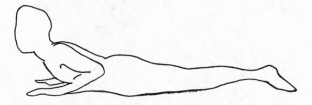

Half Locust: This is done two times with each leg. The Half Locust is a pose in and of itself, but it is also a preface to the next pose and tones the pelvic area.

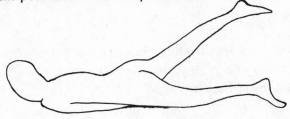

Full Locust: The Full Locust pose builds up back muscles, works on the pelvis and abdomen, and helps relieve a sluggish liver. The emphasis of this pose is on the back.

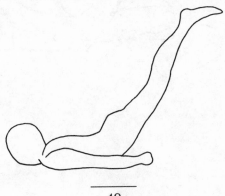

Bow Pose: This pose gives all the benefits of the Cobra and Locust poses. The emphasis is on the entire spine.

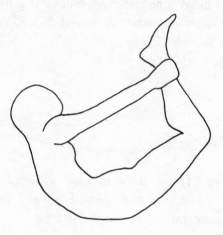

Half Forward Bending Pose: This position helps to control sexual energy. It is done once on each side, concentrating on lower back and legs.

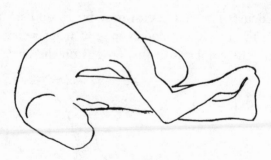

Full Forward Bending Pose: This pose stretches and exercises nearly all the posterior muscles. It is done once, concentrating on the lower back and legs.

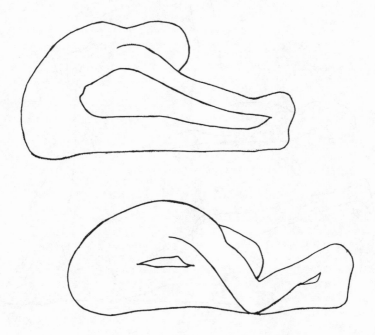

Shoulder Stand: This is done once for three to five minutes. Note: This posture should be done carefully. It should be entered into and come out of gently. Do not force it. The potential for muscular damage is great in trying to attain this position. You may use a folded blanket under your shoulders for padding, allowing your head to hang over.

Fish Pose: This pose helps relieve any stiffness of the neck caused by the Shoulder Stand. It also expands the chest cavity to help the intake of oxygen into the lungs.

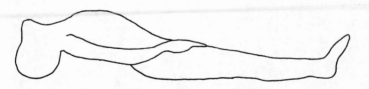

Half Spinal Twist: This is done once on each side, with emphasis on the lower spine. It strengthens the deep back muscles and helps relieve any maladjustment in the back.

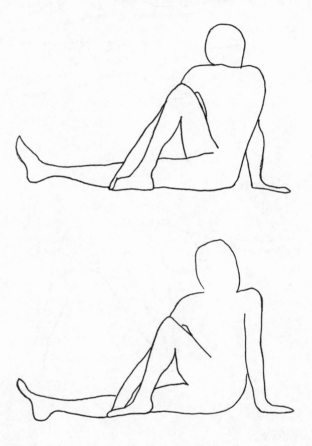

Deep Relaxation: Also known as the Corpse, this position is held for several minutes, allowing fresh energy to surge through your body. Lie flat on the floor, and release all the tension in your body. Allow the floor to support you, and follow the rhythm of your breathing for the next few minutes.

This is also a great position for lowering blood pressure.

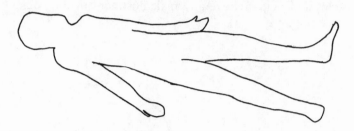

Optional Poses

Triangle Pose

Boat Pose

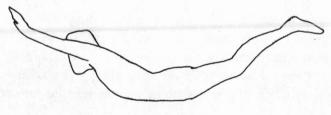

King Dancer Pose

Yoga Seal: Sit cross-legged on the floor and grasp one writst with the other hand behind your back. Bend foreward as far as possible, eventually bringing your forehead and chin to the floor. Repeat this position three to seven times and hold for ten seconds each time, working up to doing this once and holding it for two minutes.

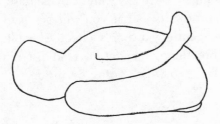

Deep Breathing: This can be practiced anytime during the day. Deep Breathing utilizes the full capacity of the lungs and allows you to take in more oxygen than with your usual shallow breathing.

It may be difficult fitting yoga into your busy days, but it's worth altering your schedule and making the time to practice. Recent research has indicated that thirty-five minutes of yoga is actually more beneficial in raising heart rate and lowering blood pressure than thirty-five minutes of brisk walking! You may feel an immediate difference after your first set of potures, but as with any physical exercise, you cannot expect imediate results. What you will begin to see and feel are the subtle, gentle, yet highly effective results of the combination of breathing, meditation, and listening with your inner guidance as to what's going on inside.

Some of the asanas can be squeezed in during a break or lunch hour at work. Some asanas don't require a lot of room and can be done anywhere—from the shower to a bathroom stall in the workplace. Others, where you may need to stretch out a bit, can be done while you're watching television or waiting for your laundry.

Here are two particularly easy postures that take only a few minutes. For the first one, you need to sit in a chair and be near a desk. This position will help ease tension and take care of your neck and lower back. Set your chair far enough away from the desk so that you can easily lean forward and still reach the desk. Sit on the edge of the chair and lean toward the desk. Cross your arms, so that each hand can comfortably grasp the opposite elbow, and rest your forehead on your arms. You can close your eyes if you like. Stay in this position for a few minutes while breathing deeply. Feel the tension slip away. When you're ready to sit up, slowly roll yourself up, one vertebra at a time, to your original sitting position.

The second position relaxes the hips, lower back, and shoulders and is especially portable because all you need is a chair. Sit on the edge of your chair and slowly lean forward, bringing your head to your knees and resting your arms at your side, letting your hands touch the floor. Again, it's best to stay in the position for a few minutes, breathing deeply.

Slowly, raise yourself up into a straight sitting position, breathing deeply as you roll out of it. CAUTION: This position isn't recommended for anyone with a sinus problem or a slipped disk.

If you have more than five minutes to spare, you can do the following postures, which I like to call "portable postures" because they can be done anywhere, without any props or a special room:

Centering
Eye Exercises
Sun Salutation
Half Spinal Twist
Deep Relaxation

Combined with some stretching and meditation, these portable postures can be a great lunch-time pick-me-up and can be done within a thirty-minute lunch period. You'll be surprised how energized and revitalized you feel, both physically and mentally.

We can all benefit by fitting yoga into our busy lifestyles. With a little creativity and lots of determination, we can help alleviate the pressures of our lives and, even if only for a few minutes a day, we can ease our tension. Go for it!

6

Weeding Out Your Doctor With Nature's Pharmacy: Herbal Medicine

Starting to get that achy feeling but don't have time to get sick? Overwhelmed by the multitude of cold and flu medicines in your local drugstore? Try some drops of echinacea with astragalis, diluted in a small glass of water or juice, every three to four hours. Your achiness will be greatly diminished, if not all gone, by the morning.

Echinacea (an extract of the cone flower that was used by Native American medicine men) is one of today's top-selling herbs. Recommending it as a remedy for achiness and cold symptoms is becoming as common as telling someone to take two aspirins for a headache. You can find echinacea in the form of capsules or tinctures—a liquid solution of the herb in an alcohol or alcohol-and-water base. (I prefer to use a tincture of any herbal remedy, if possible, because it is absorbed by the body more quickly than capsules.) The reason echinacea works so well is that it contains proteins that help non-infected cells fight infection.

So why haven't the pharmaceutical industry and the American Medical Association (AMA) cornered the market on the wonders of echinacea by patenting it and selling synthetic versions for sixty dollars a capsule? Because they can't! Herbal remedies have not undergone government testing for review of safety and effectiveness because the review process is most often costly. Since the actual plants can't be *patented* for their medicinal properties (thereby convertible into cash), there's less motivation to do research. Foods are assumed to be safe, so the herbs that are being sold to the public now are being sold as *foods* so as to not to have to undergo the regulatory testing from the Food and Drug Administration (FDA).

Just because the herbs haven't undergone government testing, however, doesn't mean they are harmful. Even medications that have been approved by the FDA can be harmful. Caution should always be taken with anything you put into your body—moderation and an awareness of what you're ingesting is very important.

With the amount of attention that herbs have been getting in the headlines recently, you would think they had just been discovered. There are ads and headlines in almost every newspaper and magazine about the beneficial aspects of ginkgo, ginseng, primrose oil, and aloe vera. In fact, the use of herbs as healing tonics, tinctures, and poultices has been going on for centuries. Unfortunately (or fortunately, depending on how you look at it), with technological advances made in chemistry and medicine, the use of herbal remedies receded in the United States into cultural pockets such as Appalachia.

Herbal healing is based on three functions: eliminating and detoxifying (laxatives and blood purifiers), maintaining (herbs used to counteract symptoms of a disease, thus giving the body a chance to heal itself), and building (herbs used to tone the organs). Each of these functions takes time to properly rectify imbalances in the body—as much as one month for each year of illness. Not only that, but it takes time to research the proper herbs to take for whatever ails you. If you get antibiotics from a doctor, they also take time, maybe not as long as one month, but you're usually given a week's supply of the medicine. Using herbal and homepathic remedies requires more work—research on what herbs are needed to combat your problem, as well as the effort of finding a good nutritionist or herbalist (though it's well worth it)—compared to just walking into your doctor's office, telling him or her you have a cold, and being handed a prescription for two weeks of antibiotics.

I believe the rediscovery and resurgence of herbs and homeopathic remedies in mainstream America is due to three main factors. The first is the slow drift away from modern medicine, with its focus on treating the *symptoms* of the disease rather than the underlying cause of the disease itself. If you develop a rash on your arm, for instance, and you treat it with cortisone cream, the rash and itchiness will recede, but you still didn't treat what *caused* the rash in the first place. The outward symptom of the disease will have seemingly disappeared, but what it really did was retreat *into* the body. Within a short amount of time, you will develop some other medical problem, such as an ache. This is not a new problem but simply a different manifestation of the original problem. By going to a nutritionist or herbalist, you will be treated with herbs that will target the imbalance in your body that caused the symptoms of the rash and ache in the first place. It's like taking an aspirin every day for a recurring headache (treating symptom, not underlying problem). You may get rid of your headache every day temporarily but it will keep coming back unless you find out what is causing it and eliminate that thing from your diet or living area (treating the cause, thus eliminating the symptom).

The two other factors I believe have led to a renewed interest in herbs are the growing desire on the part of Americans to take back control of their bodies and the high cost of health care, which forces people to look for more affordable alternatives to drugs.

As with aromatherapy, the United States is taking a slow approach to using homeopathic remedies in healing. In France and Germany, doctors in hospitals and private practice regularly prescribe herbal remedies. In Germany, echinacea is commonly prescribed for the flu, among other illnesses. A study there found that echinacea is also effective in allergy treatment because it helps prevent tissue inflammation. With results like that, it's not surprising that nearly 80 percent of the world's population relies on herbs for primary health care, according to a report by the World Health Organization.

Anything you put into your body should be taken with care, so ask a nutritionist, a naturopathic doctor, or a reputable individual with a naturopathic background to help guide you to the correct herbal remedy. Also, check packages and boxes carefully. Look for signs of tampering and expiration dates. Do not buy the remedy if it is past the expiration date or if there is no expiration date. Herbs have a shorter life span than prescription drugs so extra care needs to be taken with expiration dates. Another thing to watch out for is a fine coat of dust on the box. It's an indication of how long its been sitting on the shelf. Remember to read labels for ingredients and warnings, and if you feel a reaction to an herbal remedy, stop taking it immediately.

Be aware that not all remedies are as safe or as much of a "cure-all" as they may claim to be. The lack of testing by the FDA has left the herbal field wide open for some less-than-ethical companies to take advantage of a good thing, such as making grandiose claims for their products. I have compiled a list of herbs that have come under suspicion as being the active agent in causing illnesses. These herbs, although not banned, should be used with caution:

Chaparral: Has been used to treat cancer, colds, arthritis, sexually transmitted diseases, and cramps. In 1992, six people who ingested chaparral suffered severe liver damage.

Comfrey Root: Used as a blood purifier and to treat stomach ulcers, but evidence shows that it can cause liver cancer.

Germander: Used for weight loss. In France in 1992, several people developed hepatitis after drinking germander tea. One died.

Pokeroot: Used for arthritis, cancer, swollen breasts, and other ailments. This herb is highly toxic. It has been associated with deaths among children and severe illness among adults.

Sassafras: Promoted as a blood purifier and anti-infective, but studies indicate it's carcinogenic in rats and mice. Its use as a flavoring is now outlawed.

Remember, always investigate an herb's use to see if there are any adverse reactions and check for toxicity.

I'm not advocating that herbs take the place of a visit to the doctor, especially if you have a serious physical ailment such as a fever or bleeding. But I believe that as time goes on herbs will become more accepted and more readily available. I don't believe that they'll ever fully take the place of a visit to the doctor, or should, but herbal remedies can certainly work in conjunction with medical treatment.

The effectiveness of herbs should not be taken lightly. There have been some outstanding findings about herbal remedies used to treat serious health problems. Garlic, for example, is believed to prevent cardiovascular disease and prevent cancerous cells from forming, and is used to treat everything from high and low blood pressure and cramps to bronchial congestion and earaches, and ginseng is believed to reduce cholesterol and protect the liver from toxins. But if you have any chronic conditions, such as a heart problem or high cholesterol, it is best not to treat them with herbal remedies alone. Herbs are not magic. Used alone, they are not a cure-all. To give the best care for your body, use herbs as part of a lifestyle and immune support system that includes a low-fat diet and a low-stress lifestyle. Always see your doctor first before deciding to treat yourself if you have a serious illness, chronic condition, or are highly allergic.

Herbs come in many forms: capsules (the herb is crushed to a fine powder and put in a clear capsule tube), teas, tinctures, or extracts. The parts of the plants that are used to make these remedies are: stems, leaves, roots, flowers, or a combination of these.

Herbal remedies are a wonderful alternative to ingesting chemicals when you want to cure a physical problem. What many people don't realize is that modern medicine has gotten some of its most effective painkillers, anti-'s, and '-cillins from native plants that were found in the natural environments of the world such as jungles, ponds, streams, oceans, and meadows. Ethnobotanists travel the world to find natural plants and to learn their medicinal properties, usages, dosages, and dangers from tribal medicine men and women. Samples of the plants are collected and sent back to other scientists, who then dissect the leaf, root, stem, or flower to find the active ingredient and either chemically recreate the plants' properties or build upon the natural base remedy and add chemicals, patenting the result. Voilà! The high cost of medicine!

Valerian root, for example, a staple in any health-food store, is the ground root of the valerian plant and is used as a mild muscle relaxant and sleep aid. It is also the natural base of the drug Valium! Known as ma huang in Chinese medicine and ephedra in the West, this plant is another example of a modern medicinal plant whose roots reach back into nature. The use of this herb as a medicinal plant dates back to ancient India. But it's the Chinese species that led to the development of pseudoephedrine, which is the active ingredient in Sudafed!

I've put together a list of common herbal remedies for minor ailments along with some cautions for each. Some herbs such as echinacea, ginseng, and angelica have more than one species of plant (such as American, Siberian, Chinese, and European) and are sold under the generic name of the plant. They have similar properties, but price, availability, and effect may have an influence over which species you choose and can be found in your area. Different species of the plants, though having similar properties, may be used for different primary ailments. If in doubt as to which species of plant to choose, it would be wise to consult several herb books or ask an employee at a health-food store for help.

Astragalis: This herb is used to increase energy and build resistance to weakness and disease. It has warming properties and is a tonic to the spleen, kidneys, lungs, and blood. Astragalis is combined with other herbs in tonics to promote and enhance the other herbs' effects. It is also a good diuretic and balances the energy of all the internal organs and helps neutralize fevers and improve digestion. It's an important tonic because it strengthens the body's resistance. It is sometimes also used as a stimulant and an aphrodisiac.

Echinacea: Used to treat colds or upper respiratory viral infections, echinacea's effectiveness is based on using it as an immune strengthener. Though there are no known side effects, the tincture can have an alcohol-like taste. I always dilute the tincture in a glass of juice to kill the taste. If you buy echinacea with goldenseal, and take it continually during the day, it can upset your stomach. So, if you have a sensitive stomach, it's best to stick with pure echinacea. This herb works best at the first signs of illness and should not be used for more than seven consecutive days because when taken for a long time, it can suppress immune functioning.

Garlic: This kitchen staple is highly recommended to fight all sorts of ailments and infections, such as lung problems, headaches, and high and low blood pressure, and also helps lower cholestoral. Garlic can be ingested as fresh juice, oil of garlic, syrup of garlic, or, of course, minced and added to food. Specific ailments may call for specific forms of garlic. If you're not a fan of garlic in its natural form, capsules are available as regular or odor-free.

Ginseng: There are four varieties of ginseng—American, Siberian, Chinese, and Korean. American and Chinese ginseng are both forms of the plant *Panax ginseng*, while Siberian ginseng is actually a different plant with similar medicinal properties. Korean ginseng comes from the same plant as the Chinese ginseng, but is harvested in a different geographical area. Siberian ginseng is sold as a tea and is called a warming herb; it therefore works well for people who have poor circulation. It has also been used to help cancer patients resist the side effects of radiation therapy.

American and Chinese ginseng are used to increase energy, relieve stress, resist illness, and as an aphrodisiac. Studies of both these ginsengs indicate that they may lower cholesterol, improve athletic performance, regulate blood sugar, and protect the liver and heart from toxins. Overuse of American and Chinese ginseng can cause nervousness, insomnia, breast pain, and diarrhea.

Licorice: The root of this important Chinese herb has many beneficial properties. It is a great remedy for colds, flus, lung problems, and as a laxative. Licorice has recently gained attention for its ability to reduce the acidity in stomach ulcers and intestinal problems. You can always detect the presence of licorice in teas or tinctures because of its sweet aftertaste.

Chamomile: This herb is commonly used as a tea and can be found on any supermarket shelf. It is used for its calming effect to treat restlessness, nervousness, sleeplessness, upset stomach, and menstrual pain.

Dong quai: Often taken as a tea, this Chinese herb is an antispasmodic used to treat menstrual cramps, irregular periods, fatigue, hot flashes, and premenstrual syndrome complaints. Since this is an antispasmodic and helps regulate the flow of blood, this herb should *never* be used in any way by a pregnant woman, or a woman who is menstruating heavily.

Ginkgo: Ginkgo nuts have been used by the Chinese primarily for their effectiveness in treating asthma, bronchitis, and pulmonary conditions, while an extract of the ginkgo leaf has been found to help increase blood circulation in the body and circulation to the brain. It has also been getting a lot of attention lately as an aid to improved memory. Even a small amount of ginkgo, taken once, produces improvement and has been shown to be most effective in treating depression and age-related memory loss. The great news is that there have been no noticeable side effects with this herb.

Uva ursi, or Bearberry: This herb is used to treat menstrual bloating and the beginning of urinary tract infections. The reason it works so well in treating the *beginning* of a urinary tract infection is that certain of its compounds have been shown to interfere with bacteria adhering to the walls of the bladder and urethra. But if the urinary tract infection becomes full blown, the uva ursi must be backed up by a visit to the doctor. If a physician is not seen, and the herb is used alone to treat the infection, the bacteria can spread to the kidneys.

Ginger: Another great kitchen staple, this root eases morning or motion sickness, vertigo, and arthritis. A U.S. study found that ginger was more effective against motion sickness than the drug Dramamine! It works best when taken before vomiting begins. This herb can be taken for ailments affecting the stomach, intestines, and circulation, as well as used externally for stiff joints and muscle pain as a tea, pill, oil, or added to food in its powdered form.

Feverfew: While this herb is useful in combatting migraine headaches and treating arthritis, anyone with a clotting disorder should consult a doctor before taking it. Feverfew can also cause allergic reactions in people who are allergic to flowers.

Fenugreek: Useful for lung congestion and all mucus conditions, fenugreek is one of the oldest recorded medicinal plants. It is also an aphrodisiac and rejuvenator and is used in cooking.

Dandelion root: This common lawn intruder relieves bloating, constipation, indigestion, and colds and has been used to treat congestive heart failure. However, this herb's effectiveness has been shown more as an appetite stimulant, laxative, and general digestive aid.

Ma huang: A common ingredient in herbal weight-loss remedies because of its effect as a stimulant on the central nervous system, ma huang is also used to treat respiratory conditions such as bronchial asthma and congestion.

This herb should be used only under the supervision of a doctor because it raises blood pressure and can cause nausea, dizziness, insomnia, and heart palpitations. Though ma huang (also known as ephedra) can be found in many over-the-counter products, the FDA cannot stop the usage of this herb without proving that it is the specific cause of death or endangerment to the health of a person. In the wake of a controversy about this herb, as of this writing the FDA planned to issue warnings about excessive use of products containing ephedra.

Milk thistle: An element found in milk thistle, silymarin, has been found to protect liver cells and even to regenerate liver cells already destroyed by toxins! Milk thistle is also used to treat psoriasis. Its healing properties have been documented for thousands of years.

Saw palmetto: A small palm tree native to the West Indies and the Atlantic Coast of North America produces berries that have long been used in Europe for prostate problems, reproductive disorders, colds, urinary diseases, low libido, impotence, and also to increase the supply of mother's milk. No significant side effects have been reported. If you are going to use saw palmetto for prostate problems, use it in oil form if it is available. Consult a physician for a prostate exam.

Herbal remedies are a part of a whole field of medicine that has just begun to flower and prosper, with proven methods of healing, documented from thousands of years ago. Herbal remedies using poultices and tinctures are part of the healing knowledge of many cultures. The remedies mentioned in this chapter are only a few of the myriad that are available and can be used as tonics and nutrients to support and strengthen weakened systems in our bodies.

Homeopathic, or naturopathic, medicine is based on the following six principles.

1. The body has considerable power to heal itself. The role of the naturopathic physician is to aid this natural process by using natural, nontoxic therapies.

2. The cause is treated, not the effect. The physician seeks the underlying cause of the disease. Symptoms of illness are viewed as expressions of the body's natural attempt to heal itself, while the causes may be found in the physical, mental, and spiritual levels.

3. The physician is to cause no harm to the patient.

4. The individual is a whole, composed of the interaction of the physical, mental/emotional, spiritual, social. In this approach no disease is seen as incurable.

5. The physician is first and foremost a teacher who educates and motivates the patient to take more responsibility for his or her health by adopting a healthy attitude, lifestyle, and diet.

6. Prevention is the best cure. Prevention of disease is accomplished through education and a lifestyle that supports health.

The AMA and the pharmaceutical companies may not be whole-heartedly embracing herbal remedies just yet, but naturopathic concepts, such as a reduced-stress lifestyle, exercise, and a high-fiber, low-fat, diet, have been embraced by the general population. This is only the beginning.

As with prescription drugs, you must follow the recommended dosage when taking herbs. Just because something is all natural doesn't mean that it's okay to take a lot of it, or that the more you take, the quicker you'll feel better.

Use common sense with herbal dosages. If you have doubts, the general rule of thumb is: Use an herbal product according to the recommended dosage—one month for every year of illness.

This rule can be adjusted for shorter lengths of illness. For example, one month of illness equals approximately two weeks of using herbal remedies; a few weeks of illness equals five to ten days of using herbal remedies. Stick with the herbs for the allotted amount of time and they will work better for you in the long run. As with any medicine, do not stop taking remedies just because you feel better. You need to continue taking them for a few days after you feel better, to keep them in your system to fight off a possible relapse.

An excellent book that will teach you everything you need to know about herbs—their uses, how to make your own capsules, tinctures, and poultices—and will give you a thorough working knowledge of herbs is *The Way of Herbs* by Michael Tierra, C.A., N.D. (Simon and Schuster).

7

Stretching

Have you ever noticed the blissful look on a cat's face as it stretches? It seems to be thinking, "Ooh yeah! That feels sooo gooood."

We can learn a lot by watching cats. They instinctively know what is right for their bodies, what to eat and what not to eat, and the wrong and right ways to move. *We*, however, do not—anymore, that is. I believe we do instinctively know what is right and wrong to ingest, and the right way to move our bodies, but our consciousness and our desires have overtaken that instinct.

Stretching is a basic instinct. We stretch our muscles when we feel the need and even when we don't consciously feel the need. One moment we'll be sitting quietly and the next, before we know it, our arms shoot up through the air reaching for the ceiling, fingers flexing as a deep sigh escapes our lips. Stretching can be done everywhere and anywhere—in bed, while sitting at your desk, sitting or lying on the couch while watching television, or while listening to music.

Why Stretch?

Other than stretching to loosen our muscles as a warm-up before exercising, or to loosen tight muscles when we're tired, not much is said or written about the importance of stretching just for the sake of stretching. A lot of research has found a direct correlation between illness and a lack of physical activity, and with the increased mechanization of our homes and the workplaces, we've become a sedentary society. The shape of our bodies and the lack of strength in our muscles reflect this.

How many of us drive the five blocks to the grocery store or post office instead of walking? Machines have made our lives easier but have taken a toll on us by allowing our bodies to get soft and weak. Unfortunately, it seems as if conscious exercise has become more of an extracurricular activity than an integral part of day-to-day life.

One of the ways to get in touch with yourself on the *inside* is to get in touch with yourself from the *outside*. For those of you who have been inactive a little too long, or don't have time for exercise, stretching offers the opportunity to get in touch with your muscles in a peaceful, noncompetitive way. It can be done in any environment you choose—in the privacy of the bathroom at work, at your desk, in your bed, anywhere in your home. You don't have to go to a gym to stretch, because you don't need anything to work with but yourself.

All you require is five minutes out of your day (though longer is better) to get the benefits of these stretches. You can begin in the morning while you're still in bed, or in the evening after work. Stretching gets you in touch with your bodily rhythms. Couple it with deep breathing exercises and you will see a significant difference, over time, in your flexibility, temperament, and mental and emotional well-being.

IMPORTANT NOTE: If you have had any recent surgery or physical problems, *always* consult a physician or health care provider before beginning stretching or any other exercise program.

How to Stretch

How many people believe that a good stretch constitutes touching your toes, no matter how hard you have to bounce or how much it hurts to stretch your muscles?

You can do a stretch that way, but it's not the right way! You need to ease your muscles into a stretch. Rather than bounce until you can touch your toes, stretch until you feel the tension and tightness in your muscles. The more often you stretch, and do the stretch properly, the easier it will become. Bouncing will strain the muscles—just the opposite of what you're working toward! This is what many people do when they first begin stretching—bouncing and forcing their bodies into positions. The goal of stretching is not to reach the final position, but to flex your muscles. Even if you stretch only a little at first, it's better than not at all. Stretch as far as you feel comfortable at first. Then strive for a longer stretch. Take your time; you'll get there.

Proper breathing is essential in any kind of body work. Have you ever noticed that when you stretch, you hold your breath without being aware you're doing it? We need to be aware of our breathing and keep our breathing under control. Conscious breathing will help keep you focused. As you move into a stretch, inhale slowly, and exhale as you come out of the stretch. If you can't breathe properly while you're stretching, then you're not doing the stretch correctly. The phrase we're working with here is *not* "No pain, no gain." Instead, it's "Nice and slow will help you grow." If you stretch to the point of pain you may cause some serious damage to yourself.

There are basically two kinds of stretches we can do for ourselves: easy and developmental.

The Easy Stretch

When you begin, ease into your stretch until you feel a mild tension in your muscles, then hold your position for thirty seconds. The tension should subside as you hold the position. If it doesn't, ease back on the stretch until you feel more comfortable. The easy stretch reduces tightness in the muscles and gets your body ready for the next kind of stretch—the developmental stretch.

The Developmental Stretch

When you have become comfortable with easy stretches, it's time to begin practicing the developmental stretches. You start the same way as you would for the easy stretch, but you're going to stretch a little further until you begin to feel slight tension in your muscles. Hold for thirty seconds and (I cannot say this enough) do not bounce! The developmental stretch is great for increased flexibility.

Basic Stretches

The following four examples of stretches can be done as a series, one set immediately following the other, or can be done separately if you only have a few minutes, or just want a quick loosening up. It's entirely up to you.

1. Sit on the floor with the soles of your feet together, pulled in as close to the groin as possible, and your hands around your feet and toes.
2. Gently pull your upper body forward until you feel the stretching in the inside of your upper thighs.
3. Hold for twenty seconds.
4. Do not bend by rounding your back and pulling your head down to your feet. Move forward with your hips, keep your spine straight, and keep your chin up as if you are focusing on a spot on the floor in front of you.
5. After you feel the tension subside, increase the stretch by slowly going a little further into it. Hold for about twenty-five seconds.
6. Slowly come out of the stretch and sit up straight.
7. Breathe.

* * *

1. Sit on the floor with your right leg extended and your left leg bent so that the sole of your left foot is facing the inside of your right leg's upper thigh.
2. Do not lock your knee on the leg that is extended. Keep the knee slightly bent.
3. Bend forward from your hips (*not* by rounding your back), reaching toward the toes of your extended foot until you feel a slight tension.

4 . Hold for twenty seconds.

5. Be sure that the toes of the foot that is extended are pointing upward. This helps keep the alignment through the ankle, hip, and knee.

6. For the developmental stretch, lean a little more into it until you feel some increased tension. Again, not to the point of pain, but apply more tension than what was felt in the easy stretch. Hold for twenty-five seconds.

7. Slowly come out of the stretch and switch legs. Always remember not to bounce and to keep the toes of the foot that is extended facing upward to maintain proper alignment.

8. And *don't forget to breathe!*

* * *

1. Try this one first thing in the morning before you get out of bed. It feels wonderful! Lie on your back with the soles of your feet together. Let your knees fall apart.

2. Relax and let go of the tension in your body. Feel your hips sink into the floor.

3. Stay in this position for thirty seconds.

4. Do not push anything, let the body stretch itself!

5. Slowly, straighten both legs and reach your arms above your head.

6. As you reach with your hands and fingers, point your toes so that you're reaching and stretching at both ends of your body. This is an excellent stretch for a number of areas in your body including your abdomen, feet, chest, and arms.

7. Remember to breathe!

* * *

1. Lie on the floor with your legs straight in front of you, and your toes pointing upward.
2. Bend one knee toward your chest.
3. Hold for thirty seconds. This is a great position to stretch the lower back.
4. Straighten the bent leg and repeat with the other leg.
5. Breathe, breathe, breathe!

It's also very important to practice the proper way to get into a sitting position from a lying position, and whether from stretching, exercise, or yoga, which is to roll over onto your side with your knees bent in a fetal position and use your hands to push yourself up. This way, you are using the strength of your hands and arms instead of your back to push yourself up.

Remember to develop your stretching based on how you *feel*, not how far you can stretch. Don't over-stretch right away. And, oh yeah—breathe!

Part 2

MIND

8

Meditation in Everyday Life

"Relax! Take it easy!"

How many times has someone said this to you? (Or you to them?) My instant response used to be, "Don't tell me to relax! It's easier said than done." Well, even though it's true, of course, that it *is* easier said than done, it can still be very easy to do. All you need are a few minutes each day to devote to a calmer self. You may feel you don't have those few minutes to devote solely to meditation but you can find them: How about using the minutes spent waiting in traffic or in line at the supermarket or in front of automatic teller machines.

Relaxation through meditation, done twice a day, can really work effectively to alleviate stress. Meditation doesn't have to mean wearing white cotton garments and sitting cross-legged on the floor with eyes closed and chanting "Om" over and over. That *is* one form of meditation, but most of us don't have the luxury of time and a peaceful place to meditate that way.

Meditation is not a single practice that can be easily defined. Actually, meditation is not just something to do: It's what we used to be. As soon as we learned to talk, and words began to pour forth, our natural state of meditation was lost. The way to recapture that meditative state is to consciously bring it back into our daily lives.

The forms of meditation are diverse. There is formal sitting (vipassana), in which the body is held immobile and the attention controlled; expressive practices (siddha yoga), in which the body is set free and anything can happen; and *mahamudra*, which is a way of going about one's daily round of activities mindfully. Mahamudra is what I'll be discussing in this chapter.

Here is a simple exercise that can be done anywhere and anytime. All you have to do is *breathe!*

Begin by taking in a deep breath. Breathe in through your nose, expanding your lungs and diaphragm. Hold the breath for a few seconds and slowly exhale through your mouth. Imagine your lungs expanding as you feel the air filling them, and imagine them contracting as you exhale. Make sure you fill your lungs and diaphragm fully before you release. Repeat this three to five times (or as often as you feel necessary). You can do this with your eyes either closed or focused on some point. The focus point can be an object or a spot on the floor or wall.

The beauty of this quick release is that it can be done anywhere:

- Waiting in line at the bank or supermarket
- Sitting in the car when you're stuck in traffic or when you pick up the kids from school or practice.
- Even in the middle of your most hectic day at the office,

with phones ringing and deadlines approaching. And no one will know what you're doing.

This is similar to the classic exercise of counting to ten when you get angry in an effort to calm yourself down before you start yelling. By the time you've counted to ten, you usually feel much calmer.

If you feel as though you're getting out of touch with yourself and getting caught up in the turmoil of day-to-day living, this is a wonderful break that your mind, body, and spirit will fully appreciate. (So will the others around you, because you won't be screaming at them in frustration!)

Next time you're waiting in line at the supermarket and the clerks seem agonizingly slow, instead of scowling and tapping your foot to show your impatience, take the opportunity to do this deep breathing exercise. You'll be amazed at how quickly it can soothe the savage within us.

1. Focus on a spot on the wall or floor (or even on the back of the person in front of you).
2. Clear and quiet your mind.
3. Inhale through your nose, taking in a full, deep breath that fills your lungs and diaphragm.
4. Hold your breath for a few seconds.
5. Slowly release through your mouth, concentrating on the slowing of your breath and the beating of your heart. Consciously feel your heartbeat slow to a more restful state.
6. Repeat.

As you do this, you will notice that your mind is focused on controlling your breathing and no longer on the circumstances that annoyed you in the first place. By taking in these deep breaths, you are also allowing more oxygen into your body—an additional health benefit.

Here's an interesting experiment. Listen to your body the next time you feel stressed: You're in the car, caught in the middle of rush hour with road construction. Your car is moving at a crawl even a wounded turtle could beat. Have you noticed that your breathing has become quicker and more shallow? That your heart is pumping a little faster? That you feel a tightening in your stomach and shoulders? That your palms are damp?

Stop! You first need to realize that by feeling anxious and creating all this tension in your body, you're not going to get out of the traffic jam, or any other stressful situation, more quickly. Accept the situation, ignore the rantings of your fellow motorists, and do some deep breathing.

Acceptance is an important element in attaining that inner peace we're all looking for in this world we live in, which seems to challenge us every day. Complex situations, difficult people, and negative situations are put in front of us for a reason. Have you ever asked yourself why you seem to attract the same kinds of people, relationships, and situations in your life? We seem to get most upset about those things we need to learn about. I, myself, am guilty of reacting angrily to people who seem to know exactly how to push my buttons, by snapping at them. Most of us are in this category. But I am continually learning to accept those people and situations by stopping myself when I feel I'm getting tense and asking, Okay, what's really going on here? Why am I really getting angry and who or what am I really upset about?

A woman I once knew used to upset me because she was constantly putting down friends and coworkers while placing herself on a pedestal. I actually felt my stomach churn in disgust one day as I overheard her make severe judgmental comments about someone. Instead of staying with my own initial judgment, that she was highly opinionated and a rude snob, I looked more deeply within myself and questioned my quick response. I then closed my eyes, took some deep breaths, centered myself, and thought, Why am I getting so upset? This doesn't involve me, and no matter what I or anyone else might say, this person was not going to change. So I accepted this woman in my heart.

I even felt sorry that she found it necessary to verbally belittle her peers, and understood that she was only doing what she knew how to do. I even gave her credit for standing up for her beliefs and defending them when she was challenged by someone who would ask, "Why do you have to say that?" I immediately felt better about myself *and* this woman. This doesn't mean that she still didn't get under my skin at times. It was just a relief to be able to accept her as she was rather than heighten the problem by complaining to others about what a bitch she was. By accepting her in my heart, I felt I was contributing to lessening the animosity in our high-strung world.

Acceptance. We need to get above and beyond the annoying occurrences that always seem to surround us. We should look upon these people and situations as challenges and learn the most we can from them. It is from this learning that we'll come to know a lot more about ourselves and come to be more comfortable in our own skin. By accepting what we cannot change, we will become more acutely aware of ourselves and our surroundings, and we will open ourselves up to the inner peace and enlightenment that is just waiting to happen. It is only through acceptance, compassion, and emotional control that we will learn happiness, love, and the ability to stay centered—

focused. What is, is. This translates into a knowing—where everything feels right in our actions, thoughts, and intentions, and right about where we are at this moment in our lives. We truly begin to feel that no matter where we go, we are home because we are that comfortable in ourselves and in who we are. It is not hard to be true to yourself and still maintain a relationship with the outside world.

It's by feeling the love and peacefulness in ourselves that we are able to share it with others and create a domino-type reaction. This is the whole meaning behind the phrase "Practice random acts of kindness." Unfortunately, that phrase came to have a political connotation that turned many people off, but the idea behind it still stands: What we put out, we'll get back.

If, through meditation, we are able to calm ourselves while we're standing in that long line, and are able to feel love for those around us, and express and share that feeling with a kind word or gesture, we can help make their day and our day a little brighter. Bright enough so that the woman behind you in line may want to share a smile with someone else. And that someone else will share one with yet another—the positive domino effect.

One reality check: You are not going to be able to change everybody with a smile. Some people feel that they deserve to be let ahead in line, and some people don't realize they are no better than anyone else. You just have to remember that all people should be treated equally, and if that kindness isn't returned, then so be it—move on. You can't spend your energy on trying to be good to everyone and thinking you're going to change people with a kind word. I believe some people are so self-centered that nothing is going to change them, not even a kind word or a smile; but I like to think that such acts plant a seed. We are all like farmers, and our seeds are our acts of kindness. Some seeds will take root and grow and create a rich harvest. Some will wither and die. Still others may be carried by the wind to another part of the land and take root there. Who knows? The point is to keep trying. Just spread the kindness without expectations.

If you want to experience a little deeper meditation, try this:

1. Set your alarm clock to go off ten minutes earlier than you normally get up. (This even works for those of us who have to set the clock twenty minutes ahead just to get up on time!)

2. While the rest of the house is still asleep, and you are still cocooned in the sheets, stretch your arms and toes as far up as they will go.

3. Mentally review and "feel" every part of your body, from limbs to digits.

4. Listen to your body. Listen to the beating of your heart and the rhythm of your breathing. Focus on these rhythms, and you will become aware of a quietness in your body and mind. If thoughts of the coming day start to intrude, acknowledge them, and then quietly tell them to go away. They have no place in your head right now and you will deal with them later.

5. Concentrate on your breathing and stretch again.

Pretty soon you'll be feeling relaxed, refreshed, centered, and peaceful. There is no mystery to attaining inner peace. The key to attaining it is not held by the man behind the curtain. It's a matter of being aware—inside and out.

During meditation, you slow your body down to the point where it enters a state of deep rest, similar to when you are sleeping. Your mind is just as relaxed as your body, but the mind is still aware. You are always conscious of your surroundings. Sometimes as you begin to meditate, you will find that you cannot quiet the thoughts in your head. You can try to ignore them (in which case they will scream louder to get your attention) or acknowledge them, tell them to go away, and then refocus on your breathing. Another way to help you refocus is to use a mantra such as "Om," or some other meaningful word. Concentrate on the word as you silently repeat it to yourself with each exhale.

All it takes is a few minutes a day, a little creativity, and you have demystified meditation. You do not have to be a yogi or live in a retreat to be able to practice meditation. If you find yourself with more time and are interested in furthering your meditation practices, there are many helpful books out there that can teach you (see Suggested Reading section).

Put Your Best Foot Forward:
Walking Meditation

We've all heard about the benefits of walking, but what about the benefits of walking *meditation?*

You walk normally, as you would if you were out for a mild exercise stroll, or seeking to get from Main Street to Elm, but instead of letting your mind wander, observing the neighborhood and its residents, you focus your attention on your walk by repeating a mantra (see chapter 9) with every step, and time your mantra to the rhythm of your footsteps. Walking on loose gravel can be hypnotic (crunch, crunch, mantra,

mantra, crunch, mantra, crunch, mantra). You can adapt a walking meditation to jogging or to using a treadmill or even a stepping machine at home or in a gym.

Repeat your mantra with every step. If it has two syllables, pronounce one syllable with each step. As you do this, your point of attention will be focused within yourself, much deeper than usual, and pretty soon you won't even notice how long you've been walking or how far you've gone!

A variation on the walking mantra is to count breaths. Walk more slowly than you usually do, while breathing normally. Notice how many steps it takes for your intake of breath and how many steps for your exhale. This way, your attention is focused both on your steps and on your breathing, which pulls your mind together in a wonderful balance of peacefulness and awareness.

Oh, and, please be mindful of where you're headed. Use your mantra but be aware of your surroundings. Joggers and other walkers, and even motorists and bicyclists, may be lost in their own mantras!

9

Soul Sounds: Mantras and Affirmations

Your mind is in a constant state of flux. Thoughts are darting everywhere; from the past (the argument you had with your father twenty years ago), to the present (did you leave the coffee pot on?), to the future (there are so many things to do this weekend), and there seems to be no space in between the thoughts or any way to impose control over them.

But in actuality you *can* control your thoughts! Your mind and thoughts should not have control over you, rather you should have control over your busy mind! One of the most effective ways to do this is by slowing down and directing your thought processes through the use of a mantra.

Mantras are words and sounds of power used by Buddhists and Hindus for healing and spiritual development. They are words or expressions that have an effect upon the mind. Have you ever noticed how some phrases or words affect you more than others? The effect can be good or bad. The sound of the word(s), or mantra, is what connects you to a higher level of consciousness, and by choosing a mantra with a personal meaning behind it, you make it all the more powerful. The goal of using a mantra is to calm the mind and emotions and focus your attention to the moment at hand—to be *in* the moment.

Every religion has a mantra. One of the oldest and most popular mantras is the Hindu word *rama* (rhymes with *drama*), a word meaning "joy." Some other samples of mantras are the Eastern Orthodox *kyrie eleison;* the Islamic *Allah;* and the Christian *Ave Maria,* or simply the name of Jesus Christ. Whatever you choose, don't feel boxed in to having to use something religious. A mantra can still have meaning for you and not have a religious connotation.

Whatever mantra you choose, use it whenever you feel yourself getting angry or wound too tight. Instead of reacting with anger to a particular situation, repeat your mantra silently to yourself until calmness returns.

Eknath Easwaran, author, lecturer, and founder of the Blue Mountain Center of Meditation in Berkeley, California, has taught and lectured worldwide for more than twenty-five years on meditation and recognizing spiritual ideals. In his book *Take Your Time,* Easwaran describes how our minds can get speeded up by negative thoughts and how we can resist them.

He says, for example, that when you pass a bakery, your mind may start to repeat "danish, danish, danish" automatically, and with greater and greater urgency. Before you know it—even if you have had breakfast—you are walking out of the bakery with a danish in a little white bag. This is a time when you need to start your mantra. Keep repeating to yourself, "rama, rama, rama" (or whatever mantra you've chosen) as you near and pass the bakery.

Your mind may keep insisting "danish, danish, danish," but you need to keep thinking "rama, rama, rama." Sometimes the danish will win out, and other times not, but if you persist a day will come when you will pass that bakery by. Your mantra will have kicked right in without your having consciously called it up.

By using the mantra, we free our minds from slavery to the ego and emotion. The mantra allows us to take our attention away from what the ego is putting in front of us, which is not always good, and offers us the freedom to take a step back and make a choice.

We can also use the mantra to get our minds going when we are bored or restless. Mantras work by steadying the mind. It is extremely useful and relaxing to silently repeat our mantra when we are walking, washing dishes, waiting in line, even driving.

Selecting a Mantra

Mantras should not be selected haphazardly. It is best to choose one with which you are comfortable and have no unpleasant connotations. When I was growing up, I went to parochial grammar school and high school, and spent a few years at a Catholic college; to me, *Ave Maria* is strongly tied to memories of my school days, of going to mass every Good Friday, school uniforms, and nuns as teachers. I would feel more distracted using *Ave Maria* than comfortable because I would be distracted by the memories of my school days, but then that's my personal reaction to the church. Others of you may feel more comfortable using *Ave Maria* because of a strong and positive parochial background. It all boils down to personal interpretation and level of comfort.

A mantra should have a meaning for you. The word(s) should resonate with your being and bring your mind back into the focus of the moment. "So what?" is a mantra that works more with attention than sound, and is simple and yet unbelievably powerful. The next time you become really irritated or bothered by a person or situation, try saying "So what?" to yourself out loud or silently, repeating it in your mind. Notice how quickly that mountain of irritability is reduced to the proper perspective of a molehill in the grand scheme of things. *Akuna matada*, meaning "no fears, no worries," is another wonderful, uplifting, and quite catchy phrase I've heard a number of people use ever since the release of Disney's *The Lion King*. The amazing thing I've noticed with mantras is that by continually repeating them, the impact they can have on refocusing your thought processes is phenomenal.

Once you have chosen your mantra, *stick to it*. Every repetition of your mantra will take you a little deeper into yourself, so it's important not to keep changing words.

Affirmations

Caregivers in the health industry long ago recognized that many physical ailments stem from people's emotional and mental outlook. Your self-image will affect your physical state whether you realize it or not. If you're feeling bad about yourself or a situation you're in, your posture slumps, the muscles in your face become drawn, and you speak in a lower tone without the usual inflection. Even the colors and types of clothing you wear when you're not feeling good about yourself advertise your emotional condition. When you feel confident and good, you stand up straighter and tend to smile more. Your physical and mental posture improve dramatically.

Positive affirmations will help you change your outlook about yourself and even your surroundings. Just as you can come to believe negative statements about yourself, you can come to believe positive ones. We all have those old tapes that play in our heads: "I'm not good enough," "I'm lousy at baseball," "I'm too anxious." We need to turn these negative mental thoughts around and reprogram them in a positive way, without adding qualifiers such as *should, maybe,* or *sometimes.*

Instead of saying "I'm lousy at baseball," say "I am doing my very best to play this sport"; instead of "I'm too anxious," say "I'm peaceful and relaxed." The emphasis should be on the state you *desire* to be in. For example, "My back feels strong and healthy today," instead of "My back doesn't hurt today." This change in emphasis makes a big difference in your mental outlook. Some people might say it's only a matter of semantics, but when you say that something *isn't* occurring, then you are not really dealing with what's at hand.

When you put your statements in a positive frame, however, you are not ignoring the situation/illness: you are creating an opportunity for a new circumstance to arise—a new attitude. These statements can be repeated as often as you like and for as long as you like—from five minutes to half an hour. They are most productive after a meditation, but you can also repeat your affirmations throughout the day.

A wonderful author to read who has delved deeply into creative visualization in her studies of psychology and human development and the powerful effects visualization can have in our lives is Shakti Gawain. (See the Suggested Reading section of this book for more information.)

Stress Busters

- Doodle
- Close your eyes for a minute and revel in the darkness. Take four or five *deep* breaths, exhaling slowly.
- Give yourself a five-minute foot massage.
- Constant interruptions and phone ringing? Take two minutes and completely dissociate from your surroundings. Let the "noise" wash over you, not through you.
- Go outside for a walk around the block, or even a walk in the parking lot at your office, for a change of scenery and completely different atmosphere.
- S-T-R-E-T-C-H.
- Think about how much you've already accomplished during your day instead of dwelling on what still needs to be done. (For some of us, just getting out of bed can be an accomplishment!)
- Watch the clouds go by and imagine what it would be like to touch one.
- Remember the games you liked to play as a child and play one again!
- Buy a plant and nurture it until it's the biggest, healthiest plant you've ever had. If you're the type who can kill even a cactus (like me), try to look at the plant as something that's alive instead of just another thing that you have to water.
- Go to a playground and sit on a swing. Start swinging, remembering what it felt like when you were a child to have the sun on your face and the wind brushing past your ears as you tried to swing higher and higher, and your only care in the world was how high you could go!

- Take a box of crayons, colored pencils, or pastels and some plain white paper, and just draw whatever comes to mind. Don't look at the clock or answer your phone. You'll quickly notice the tension shipping away.
- Take a luxurious bath or shower.
- Go to bed a little earlier or take ten minutes out of your schedule and read a passage from your favorite book, a poem, or an inspirational passage, and reflect on it during the day.

10

Mudras: Getting in Touch

Even Disney has gotten into the act! If you look closely at Rafiki in a scene from *The Lion King*, you will see that he is sitting on a rock in the classic Lotus yoga position, his arms outstretched and his fingers curled in the prana mudra position. (Stick with me; I'll explain later.) I like to call mudras a gentle yoga. The word *mudra* may sound mysterious, but there's no mystery behind it. It's taken from Hatha yoga and means "healing finger postures." Western practitioners of hatha yoga are familiar with mudras, but even those of us who are not practitioners may be familiar with the poses from pictures we have seen depicting holy scenes (stained glass windows in Catholic churches, for instance).

I use the word *gentle* because a mudra is a healing posture that can be done "softly" without anyone knowing what you're doing. It's no fuss, no big to-do, and can be done anywhere, anytime, and literally anyplace—kind of like breathing exercises while you're standing in line at the bank—and yet it can be remarkably calming or exhilarating, depending on which posture you do.

As with any health practice, keep in mind that using mudras is not a replacement for going to see a health practitioner—holistic or Western. As already stated, yoga philosophy pictures the individual as a reflection of the greater universe. The purpose of doing yoga exercises is to bring the mind and body into harmony with the universal energy (life force) called *prana*. Remember, the body and mind should work together. They are *not* enemies in constant battle with each other as they often seem to be.

The Five Elements

By picking up this book, you have taken the first step into a new world of thinking. As with all yoga, the belief is that our body contains the five elements: fire, or energy; air; sky; earth; and water. And each of our five fingers represents one of these elements:

1. Thumb = Fire, or energy
2. Index finger = Air
3. Middle finger = Sky
4. Ring finger = Earth
5. Little (pinky) finger = Water

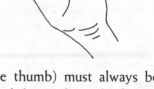

In all of these mudras, fire (the thumb) must always be included. Mudras use a system of lightly touching the fingertips, knuckles, or base of the fingers to the thumb continuously for a period of about forty-five minutes to produce those vital elements. It is a scientific fact that the fingertips contain certain nerve endings, so if you are sensitive and practice the mudras often, you'll begin to feel the current. It's great, and it actually works!

Please note that each of the mudras should be done for at least forty-five minutes at one time, using both hands. Two thirty-minute periods will also work well. If you cannot use both hands (because you are reading a book or writing), you can do the mudra with the hand not being used. But try doing it during your walking meditation, while watching television, or even at the movies (when your hand's not in the popcorn bag!). Any activity that doesn't require the constant use of your hands is a perfect time to employ the mudras.

Prana Mudra: For Overall Health

Prana mudra is used for general health, eye weaknesses, and all life-threatening illnesses. The word *prana* means "life force" in Sanskrit; therefore, this is the mudra most often recommended for general health.

Bringing together the three fingers that are used in this mudra starts special energy flowing that will rejuvenate the whole body. The body gets "charged" and begins to function properly again because the *prana*, or life force, starts flowing inside the body with a tremendous force.

Practicing the prana mudra helps activate the immune system, and, as with all of these mudras, the more it is practiced, the better is the result.

How You Do It

Lightly touch together the tips of the thumb (fire or energy), the ring finger (earth), and the little finger (water).

Surya Mudra: For Coming Alive

Surya mudra is used to rid the body of lethargy. *Surya* means "sun" in Sanskrit. In this posture, which is used when the body feels heavy or lethargic, the thumb and ring finger create a different kind of electrical impulse than in the prana mudra. Surya mudra promotes lightness, and it is believed that by using this mudra, one starts to acquire mystical power.

How You Do It

First, touch the tip of the ring finger (earth) to the base of the thumb (fire). Then curl the thumb over the knuckle of the ring finger.

Varun Mudra: For Dryness

Varun means "water" in Sanskrit, and this mudra is designed to rectify all the problems related to lack of sufficient water in the body, such as dryness or blood impurities.

Your body is approximately 70 percent water. If you do not have enough water in your body, your system gets out of balance and this can cause dehydration and kidney problems; the body can also become overacidic, creating other illnesses. This is a good mudra for people with kidney problems, stiffness, and impure blood.

How You Do It

This is one of the easiest mudras to do. Simply touch the tip of the little finger (water) to the tip of the thumb (fire or energy).

Linga Mudra: For Generating Heat

Linga mudra uses all of the fingers of both hands and spreads heat throughout the entire body. This mudra is also good for any kind of chest weakness. When you feel cold, it will bring warmth to your whole body. It's also helpful for those with chronic coughs and colds. Done with patience, over a period of time, it will bring results. Remember: Nothing brings instantaneous relief.

How You Do It

Place both palms together. Then clasp the fingers of the right hand with the left hand in such a way that you keep only the left thumb sticking straight up. The thumb and index finger of the right hand clasp the left thumb tightly, then close the other fingers around the left hand.

Jnana Mudra: For Gaining Wisdom

Jnana mudra is called the wisdom posture because *jnana* means "knowledge" in Sanskrit. This is the hand posture shown in most statues of Buddha. If you do no other mudras, this is the one you should make an effort to practice. It is a posture that generates harmony, peace, bliss, and knowledge of the universe that is beyond our conscious understanding. This mudra also increases the flow of blood to the brain and helps increase brain power and memory retention.

How You Do It

Lightly touch together the tip of the thumb and index finger. This brings together the elements of fire and air, a powerful combination.

Bayau Mudra: For Easing Pain

Bayau means "air" in Sanskrit, making this an excellent mudra for helping rid the body of joint pains like arthritis. This mudra is designed to help the vital air in the body flow properly.

How You Do It

The thumb (fire) and the index finger (air) are used again, but in a different position. The index finger lightly touches and presses the base of the thumb. The thumb then curls over and lightly presses the knuckle of the index finger. For best

results, alternate this mudra with the
prana mudra explained earlier.

Prithvi Mudra: For Renewing Energy

Prithvi mudra is used for increased bodily energy and flexibility of mind. In Sanskrit, *prithvi* means "earth." When fire
touches earth, the energy of the body starts charging. By the
renewed flow of energy, the part of the body lacking nour-
ishment starts getting it. This posture greatly helps when
there is a weakness in the body due to lack of vitamins.

Prithvi mudra also helps to promote flexibility of the
mind—to help one become more open minded. This is also
the mudra whose practice leads to the experience of different
kinds of bliss.

How You Do It

Touch the tip of the thumb (fire, or
energy) to the tip of the ring finger
(earth).

Mudras can be used for shorter periods of time with some
results, but, as with any practice, the benefit you'll receive is
equal to the time spent doing it. Use these mudras as often
as needed.

11

Seeing the Light: Candle Meditations

Praying with fire is a practice that began long ago with primitive peoples. As one of the strongest elements, fire can wipe out any given area while simultaneously cleansing it. It is warming, but it can also burn. Fire is not something to be taken lightly. It needs to be properly understood. A very powerful tool, candle meditation, utilizing the power of fire, is used for visualizations and calming the inner self. The flame actually represents the inner self.

Have you ever noticed that sometimes we feel lonely even when we're surrounded by people? The reason for this is simple, and yet can have a serious effect on our well-being. We've lost touch with the Earth and with our connection to its vibration that humans have communicated with since they began populating this planet. One wonderful way to recapture this energy is through candle meditation. No matter how you look at it, there is something primal about a fire. Even a gentle, flickering flame contains the potential for great harm if it's not respected and controlled. How many times have you heard the warning *Never leave a candle unattended?* That tiny glow can cause a house to burn to the ground. We should never underestimate the power of a flame—even that of a candle.

Candles are used in all sorts of ceremonies, and for magic and casting spells, but they are also used as a powerful tool in meditation. The wonderful thing about candle meditation is that you don't have to sit in front of the candle and do a full meditation to receive the benefits of candle healing. Candles can be lit and kept within view as you're cooking dinner, watching TV, or reading. Having a candle in the background can serve not only as a reminder to meditate but as a representation of the fire element. Candles can be both strengthening and soothing. There's something Old World and romantic about a lit candle. It evokes a sense of mystery.

The color of a candle plays an important role in attaining your desired result, as does its scent. Lighting a candle scented with jasmine or roses can help facilitate your meditation. It smells great, too!

The following is a list of candle colors and their healing abilities. Choose a candle in the color appropriate for what you'd like to attain, and light it for a few minutes each day until your desire comes true. For example, suppose you are looking for a new apartment. You would light a brown candle, the color representing grounding and dwelling, while concentrating on finding that new place. Light it every day until you get news of a new apartment. And don't forget to check the real estate ads!

Light Blue: Psychic ability and compassion.

Each of us has psychic abilities we can tap in to, and light blue is traditionally associated with psychic powers. It is also a good color to use with meditation and for getting in touch with our intuitions and gentle emotions. If you have closed off your heart because you were hurt in the past, you can use a light blue candle to get in touch with your tender side again.

Blue: Serenity, inner peace, increasing intuition, healing, tranquility, and forgiveness.

A feeling of inner peace is one of the best gifts you can give to yourself. It is one of the essential ingredients for a happy, balanced life. Meditating with a blue candle helps us get in touch with that area of inner balance.

Navy Blue: Harmony, understanding, and truth.

Silver Blue: Deep wisdom, intuition.

Sea Green: Emotional healing and protections, and calming.

Light Green: New beginnings, and looking and feeling younger.

Light green is the color of new life in the spring. This color is often used for bringing about a feeling of rebirth and renewal.

Green: Healing, money, prosperity, luck, fertility, and abundance.

Turquoise: Awareness, meditation, and creativity.

Yellow: Clairvoyance, learning, mind, communication, happiness, luck, and intelligence.

Each of us has an untapped level of knowledge in which answers to questions can be found. By using a yellow candle we help unlock and tap into that deep web of knowing found in our unconsciousness, dreams, and inner voice.

Red: Love, passion, energy, enthusiasm, and courage.

All shades of red are the color of love! Use red to help attract love in your life—a life partner, lover, the love of friends and family—or to unleash the love in your heart for yourself!

Rose: Self love, and enhancing friendships.

Orange: Strength, authority, attraction, joy, success, positive thoughts, and cheerfulness.

Peach: Gentle strength and joy.

Pink: Emotional love, friendships, caring, tenderness, harmony, and affection.

It's important to remember that emotional love doesn't always mean romantic love. Burning a pink candle opens us to the communal kind of love found in friendships and the love for all living things.

Purple: Confidence, success, career enhancement, spirituality, wisdom, and psychic awareness.

Lavender: Intuition, dignity, and spirituality.

Brown: Strength, stability, and acquiring land.

A brown candle is perfect for tapping into our inner reserves for strength, stability, practicality, and self-discipline because brown represents the Earth—and you need to be *grounded* in order to be able to effectively draw upon your strength. This is also an excellent color to use if you're looking for a place to move to, or are interested in acquiring land.

Black: Transformation, magic, subconscious wisdom, absorption and destruction of negative energy, and change.

The color black represents many things to many people. Primarily, in Western culture, it's looked upon as a color of mourning or great seriousness, even evil, but to others it represents the hidden, deep subconscious mind, or repressed memories and old fears. It also holds the seeds of creativity yet to be unleashed! It is like the night—ready to give itself up to a bright, new day!

White: Protection, peace, purity, truth, harmony, and spiritual attainment.

White has always been associated with a supreme level of purity, so to attain our highest level of vibrational energies, intent, and spiritual attainment, meditating on a white candle is highly recommended.

Let Us Begin

Sit in a dark room—or a room that is dimly lit—and take in your hands a candle of the color you wish to work with. Natural beeswax candles are considered most effective because they are made up of completely natural materials, and they come in the same variety of colors as other wax candles. If you do not have beeswax candles, or cannot get them, don't worry, any candle will work fine.

As you sit holding the candle, close your eyes and take three deep breaths. If there is something specific you wish to meditate on, let a picture of the object or a particular feeling enter your mind. Open your eyes. If there is nothing specific, then just clear your mind, place the candle in a holder, and light it.

Now, sit back and stare into the flame for a few minutes. Notice the colors of the flame, the way it dances and grows tall and thin, and then becomes short and squat. Be conscious of every breath you take, every itch you long to scratch, and the warmth of the room. Let your conscious mind drift as your unconscious mind "talks" with the flame. If you had a specific picture of your intent in your mind, dive into it and imagine actually living that desire. Imagine every facet of it. Continue to sit comfortably in front of the candle for as long as you like and just relax and enjoy its glow. Don't worry about how long this is taking. Candle meditations have no time limit—no meditation does. Simply do your candle meditation for as long as you feel comfortable.

It is important to remember with all kinds of meditation that change will not happen if you are not helping to create the change in your conscious life. For example, you may decide to try meditation to slow down and get some peace in your life—physical and mental—but you continue to eat junk food, drink alcohol, and stay up late. And even though you meditate, you notice that you still feel the same. When you meditate, you are essentially asking the energy of the Universe to help you. You cannot expect the Universe to bring you energy for work that needs to begin with you. This belief is even immortalized in Benjamin Franklin's adage, "God helps them that help themselves." Have faith, whether you believe in God, Atman, the Holy One, or whatever you call the energy, but don't expect miracles without a little help from yourself. Also, don't begin any kind of meditation thinking that your problems will be solved next week. To help maintain the necessary patience, I always say that the problems we encounter in our lives and in ourselves happen for a reason: they are opportunities for learning and growth.

As with anything in life, we cannot expect other people to solve our problems for us. We must take responsibility for ourselves, our own problems, and find our own solutions.

Caution: Always be sure to keep the lit candle away from children and flammable objects, and be sure that it is snuffed out completely at the end of your meditation. Traditionally, in candle meditations and prayers, a candle is never blown out, but is pinched or extinguished with a candle snuffer. When using any of the four elements—earth, water, fire and air—in prayer or meditation, it's considered a sign of disrespect to the four elements to mix them. So, if you blow out a candle, you're really mixing the elements of fire and air.

Above all, enjoy the quiet time with your candles. Remember: Your inner peace will equal the effort you put into it.

12

Rainbow to Go: Color Healing

Color healing is an easy yet effective and therapeutic method of incorporating colors and the body's ability to self-heal. All seven bands of the rainbow contain healing properties. There have been many articles written on how color affects humans and animals mentally and emotionally. Articles in home-decorating magazines advise readers that in order to create a calm and relaxing atmosphere in a room, paint or decorate in shades of blue, green, or white. These are colors that heal the psyche. Red, on the other hand, is an energetic color and is rarely recommended for bedroom walls! Red stimulates the brain and evokes tense feelings. It can also play a role in elevating blood pressure.

There's more to this method of healing than just wearing a certain color and deciding, "This will cheer me up today," or, "Red always makes me feel better." So how does color healing work? All atoms in the universe vibrate at different frequencies, and each color (light wave) also vibrates at a different frequency. When you look at a particular color, it stimulates your body's atoms in the areas most sensitive and responsive to that particular color's vibration. The atoms' vibrations work with and off of each other. True healing occurs when there is a change in mental attitude or belief, because long-term, beneficial healing begins from the inside.

The colors themselves do not do the healing, but the vibrations of their atoms give the body that needed spark to perform its own healing. To put it another way, color healing is based on the law of attraction. The colors are broken down into two categories: hot and cold. There are three hot colors (red, orange, and yellow) and three cool colors (blue, indigo, and violet). Green is not categorized because it exists alone as a balancing, harmonious color at the center.

Each color corresponds to a particular energy center (chakra) in the body and has its own specific healing property. For example, the red ray corresponds to the center of the body at the base of the spine; yellow corresponds to the solar plexus; green is a color balancer and is the color of the heart center; while violet, the highest vibrational color, is used by healers to ease birth and death transitions.

Of all the different types of healing, color healing is one of the most adaptable. Its versatility lies in the user's being able to take advantage of color healing properties using any medium. You can exercise color healing by painting a room a certain color or simply by wearing an article of clothing in a healing color.

Since not all of us have the capability or resources to redecorate our homes according to the colors that would energize or soothe us, what we can do instead is incorporate any color's healing process through the clothes we wear; through decorating our homes with objects in the appropriate colors such as candles, sheets, lamp shades, frames, flowers; and even through cooking! A platter bursting with red, green, and yellow food will stimulate you more than a bowl of beige oatmeal. Next time you go to your supermarket's vegetable aisle, be aware of the various colors. Don't think about what the vegetable is, but make your selection based on the deep greens and purples, bright yellows and oranges and reds, colors that attract you, and see what kind of dish you can make!

The following is a list of colors, their healing properties, and the areas of the physical body they stimulate. Let your imagination run wild on ways of bringing the effective use of color healing into your life.

Red

Healing Properties: Warmth. Red gives off a healing, vitalizing, and stimulating vibration.

Areas of Physical Stimulation: Red stimulates the liver. It increases the circulation and warms the entire body, and helps to clean out mucus and waste from the body. It corresponds with the center of the body at the base of the spine. Red is also good for problems with the bladder, poor circulation, hemorrhoids, menstrual cramps, problems with reproductive organs, and for general physical strength.

Orange

Healing Properties: Warmth and stimulation.

Areas of Physical Stimulation: Orange stimulates the lungs and is helpful in raising the energy level in general. Problems with the kidneys, lower colon, and spleen can be helped by this color. It also relieves gas, convulsions, and cramps throughout the digestive system.

Yellow

Healing Properties: Warmth. Yellow cleanses and purifies the entire body system. It also has a soothing effect on nerves and influences the higher consciousness and soul.

Areas of Physical Stimulation: Yellow corresponds to the solar plexus and stimulates the liver and all the other organs in the body except the spleen. It also increases the appetite and assists in the assimilation of food. Using yellow as a healing color is most effective in chronic conditions. It loosens and eliminates mucus throughout the entire body and allows for clearer and more positive thinking. It's a definite "feel good" color.

Green

Healing Properties: Cooling. Green is a very important color. Its vibration balances all the emotions and the mind and gives new energy and stimulation. Color healing should start with one or more exposures to this potent color.

Areas of Physical Stimulation: Green is believed to dissolve blood clots and build muscles. It stimulates the pituitary gland for better control of other glands and organs throughout the body. It also helps heal asthma, emphysema, heart problems, and other problems in the lungs and bronchial tubes.

Many years ago, some sanitariums in Europe were built in areas that were surrounded by trees and rolling hills and fields because it was believed that the color green calmed the mind and nerves and helped facilitate mental healing. Try keeping lots of plants around the house—even one on your desk at work. If you don't have a green thumb, try silk plants instead.

Blue

Healing Properties: Cooling. This color is widely recognized as evoking calm, peaceful, and cooling vibrations and feelings.

Areas of Physical Stimulation: Blue is useful in inducing sleep and relaxation and effectively relieves stress. This color's vibration can be applied as a tonic to relieve inflammation, inward bleeding and nervousness, as well as to relieve allergies, asthma, emphysema, burns, cuts, headaches, lymph problems, rashes, toothaches, thyroid problems, and lung and bronchial tube congestion.

Indigo

Healing Properties: Cooling. Indigo is considered of great value in treating certain forms of nervous and mental disorders. It is also used for attaining spiritual growth and for releasing unwanted habits and emotions.

Areas of Physical Stimulation: This is one of the most popular colors used by homeopaths to treat lung diseases. Indigo is also used to treat cuts, ear aches, eye problems, headaches, infections, and to kill germs in general.

Violet

Healing Properties: The healing in this color affects the vibration of the brain, mental processes, and spiritual aspects in each of us. It has a very high vibrational rate and is best suited for those who want to express themselves in a creative area. It also carries a high psychic vibration.

Areas of Physical Stimulation: The brain and hair growth. This is a strong color to use if you're trying to develop your ESP.

White

White is a color that is not of the rainbow but is still very important. To surround yourself with white indicates a desire for purity and universal healing. A wonderfully enriching and easy way to get the full effect of this color is to wallow in early morning sunlight for a few minutes.

13

Stones and Gems:
Nature's Jewelry Store

Almost everywhere you look nowadays you see gems and crystals in stores, sold loose, incorporated in jewelry, or crafted into geometric or animal shapes. Crystals and gems have become staples of the New Age community. These earthly delights have been used for hundreds of years in sacred ceremonies, as conductors of energy vibrations, and for healing. Remember crystal radios? And now the use of stones for healing and attunement, instead of simply for decoration, has come back into the modern world with a vengeance.

Some people think that in order to achieve higher consciousness you must *choose* a crystal. Just the opposite is true. The crystal chooses *you*. If a crystal drops in front of you, or falls off the shelf, it is trying to get your attention. That crystal will be an ally and guide in the areas in which you need help—whether you're conscious of the need or not. This can mean a physical healing or a moving onward to the next higher level of consciousness through realizations and awareness.

As an experiment, pick up any crystal and be open to whatever feelings come to you. You may notice that the crystal becomes hot to the touch, or that it remains cold. This occurs because crystals have electromagnetic energy, as does the human body (as does the entire universe), and when a natural quartz crystal comes in contact with any part of the body, it is capable of drawing out any imbalanced energy. The crystal will then change temperature as it absorbs the imbalanced energy. The temperature will change to hot or cold depending on the individual's response/rapport with the crystal. One person may feel warmth, and another iciness. If a crystal is given to you, and you don't think you can benefit from its healing properties, accept the crystal anyway, for there may be a healing process—physical, emotional, or mental—that you may not be consciously aware of; the Universe, however, meant that crystal to find its way into your life.

To facilitate physical healing, sit or lie comfortably in a quiet place and hold the gemstone in your hand or on the afflicted area for a few moments. Practice deep breathing techniques as you hold the crystal and let it work on you. If you want to *receive* the benefits of any gemstone, try holding it on your left side (hands, pocket). If you wish to *protect* a specific quality, keep the stone on your right side. If I want a total body healing or protection, I've found it beneficial to carry a gemstone with me either in my pocket, around my neck, or somewhere else on my person, either molded into jewelry or as a loose stone. There are many necklaces, earrings, and bracelets that are made nowadays with gems such as tiger's eye, malachite, and turquoise that are quite beautiful.

Crystals are nature's jewels and our primal teachers. Be open to their energies and listen to what they have to say. The following is a list of gems and crystals that are used to aid in the healing of physical ailments.

Amethyst: depression, headache, habit breaker
Bloodstone: blood problems, childbirth
Bloodstone (silver): hepatitis
Chrysocolla: asthma/breathing, diabetes
Citrine: jaundice, general internal, liver, stomach, hepatitis
Diamond: memory
Fluorite: menopause, tumors
Green turquoise: weight
Hematite: kidneys, multiple sclerosis
Herkimer: memory
Jasper: childbirth
Red jasper: impotence
Lapis: immune system, throat
Malachite: arthritis, muscular problems, tumors
Moonstone: hair loss
Peacock ore: cancer
Rose quartz: heart problems, menopause
Tourmaline: memory

Gems and crystals can be beneficial for emotional as well as for physical healing. The same techniques for tapping into their properties are used for both. The following is a list of stones that will aid in emotional healing and protection.

Aqua aura—inner peace
Aquamarine—safe travel
Agate—emotional grounding

Amethyst—protection
Ametrine—repairing the aura
Aventurine—luck
Bloodstone—healing
Carnelian—physical well-being
Citrine—alleviating fears
Chrysocolla—emotional stress
Crystal—intuition
Diamond—fidelity
Fluorite—transition
Garnet—energy
Geodes—fertility
Hematite—protection (from others' energy, emotional bombardment)
Herkimer diamond—new beginning
Howlite—communication
Jasper—physical grounding
Lapis—wisdom
Malachite—removing spiritual block
Moonstone—sensitivity
Moss agate—energy cleaner
Onyx—protection
Pearls—patience, femininity
Peridot—money
Petrified wood—past lives
Quartz, rutilated—direction
Rhodocrosite—rescues rescuers
Rose Quartz—love
Ruby—self-love
Tiger's-eye—opportunity
Blue turquoise—stress
Green turquoise—metabolism

Although, as I mentioned earlier, gems have always been around, the more popular precious ones—diamonds, rubies, emeralds—have held the spotlight until recently. Now, turquoise, onyx, and lapis are enjoying the attention with a tremendous increase in popularity, especially with Southwest and Native American designs.

The role that gems have played in our lives is exemplified by the advertising phrase "A diamond is forever." Diamond rings are common as tokens of engagement and "true love," and why not? Diamonds represent fidelity, after all. And aren't pearls considered to be a token of ultimate femininity? How many of us played with our mother's pearl necklaces when we were little girls, pretending to be grown up? How many of us were given a pearl necklace at a special event in our lives—such as graduation or an eighteenth birthday? Gems always seem to hold a special place in our lives and have been used as tokens of commemoration and celebration.

Do gems and crystals and stones really work? The only limit to the power of these gems is our own doubt, inhibition, and lack of imagination. Gems and crystals were originally incorporated into pieces of jewelry because their power and beauty were recognized, and that power was best utilized when it was constantly near the wearer, the idea being that the stone could be constantly close to the body. Only later did the idea of their healing powers emerge. It was eventually learned that energy can be increased or decreased depending on what kind of jewelry is worn and on what part (appendage and side) of the body. The belief is to wear the gem/jewelry on the left side to receive the properties and on the right to project healing outward.

Metals are also believed to be good conduits for energy. Silver, for instance, receives energy. Gold sends energy. Platinum is neutral. Copper conducts energy. There have been studies showing that people with diabetes, who wore copper bracelets for a period of time, needed less insulin than another group of diabetics who didn't wear any copper.

To get the greatest benefit from wearing jewelry, apart from its beauty, keep this in mind: Necklaces have an impact on personality, pendants have an impact on dreams and desires, and—my favorite—earrings complete a circuit of energy around your body, when they are worn symmetrically.

Rings have a definition all their own. Rings worn on the thumb represent the wearer's will and desire; rings on the index finger represent the wearer's direction and action; rings on the middle finger represent the wearer's intuition and inspiration; rings on the ring finger represent the wearer's creativity; and rings on the pinky finger represent change or opportunity for the wearer. The projection and receiving of the energies from your rings is the same as for using the gemstones. Wear them on the left side of your body to receive and on the right to project. Trust in the gems, open your heart and mind to them, respect them, and treat them well.

Gems and crystals need to be cleansed after you purchase them, and after they are worn or handled on a regular basis. Cleansing removes any negative energies that may have accumulated throughout the day.

Two of the easiest ways to cleanse your stones are to place them in direct sunlight for a few hours (a windowsill would be fine), or to treat them with burning sage (a well-known cleansing herb), allowing smoke from the smoldering sage to envelop the crystal or gem for a few minutes. It is important to make sure that the cleansing process is done with the clearest and worthiest intentions in your heart.

Treat and use your piece of Mother Earth with great joy and respect and you will benefit greatly.

Part 3

SOUL

14

Checking It Out

Rarely do we take enough time in our day to see how we are doing. We are always rushing around, if not physically, then mentally, worried about how everyone else is doing, or what we have to do next. As a counterbalance to this frantic lifestyle, there is a wonderful technique I learned that will give you access to the inner workings of your mental, emotional, and physical bodies in a short amount of time. This exercise takes only a few minutes and can be done anywhere, but in the beginning it would be helpful if you could find a quiet space for five minutes, even if it means retreating to your bathroom. It will add a nice break in the day and really gets you in touch with various aspects of yourself. You may find that your body, mind, and soul will reveal things you haven't heard before, because you either weren't listening or didn't know how to listen—until now!

First take a few deep breaths and be aware of the present: the way you are sitting, the way you are breathing, the temperature of the room. Let your worries and the accumulated tension of the day fall away. Focus on whatever you feel is going on inside of you. Don't dwell on what you have to do later. Check in with your mind: Notice what words or thoughts are predominant. Once you recognize, or "hear," your thoughts, just acknowledge them. Don't feel you have to "do something" about them.

Next, check in with your emotions. What is the overwhelming feeling in your emotional body? Sadness? Joy? Confusion? Follow whatever feeling arises. The depth of the emotion you're feeling may surprise you. If a feeling comes up that's frightening or mystifying, stay with it and breathe into whatever it is. Don't run away from it. It's only by facing our fears and emotions head on that we can begin to understand ourselves and our lives.

Finally, feel your body. Does your attention get drawn to a particular area? What emotion do you feel, if any, when you focus on that area? Again, if some emotion comes up such as fear, anxiety, or anger, breathe into that emotion. Become one with it and delve into its depths and into any physical discomfort you may feel.

If nothing comes up in any of the three check-ins, sit and listen to the sounds around you. Listening is the key. The point of this exercise is to learn to become aware of yourself and your inner and outer worlds. Too many illnesses—emotional and physical—are the result of not paying attention to what's going on inside of us.

A person who experiences sadness during the emotional check-in, for example, can work on that emotion and begin to deal with it on a more aware level. Even if the sadness is labeled as nothing more than a gnawing feeling, and not identified as actual sadness, it can eventually grow into a deep depression if not acknowledged. But by allowing ourselves to recognize the forces of emotions at work within each one of us, we can advance in self-awareness and emotional health.

You can practice this check-in on line at the supermarket, waiting at the laundromat, or even in the privacy of a public bathroom during a hectic, hair-pulling work day. Use your creativity. Sometimes nothing will come up, other times you may be surprised at what *does* come up! Either way, don't be disillusioned or discouraged!

15

One-Pointed Attention

Have you ever eaten a meal while watching television, ready to take the next bite, and realized that your plate was empty? You felt as if you hadn't eaten anything at all and couldn't remember eating the last bite. Have you ever spent an evening with your spouse or significant other, when, at the end of the night you looked at the person, almost with surprise, and were overwhelmed by a sense that you were looking at him or her for the first time that night?

We've all experienced some version of these scenarios—of losing track of where we are and what we're doing. It's not a matter of forgetfulness or even of being preoccupied with something. It's more a case of lacking one-pointed attention. Most of us spend a great deal of time either lost in memories of the past or thinking about what we have to do tomorrow or later that day. Whether we realize it or not, this lack of attention to the present reduces our quality as people because we are not giving our complete and full attention to those around us.

It is important to devote one-pointed attention to the people around us. Instead of just hearing someone's words, look into their eyes, watch their mouth forming the words, hear the inflection of the words, and reach out for the emotion behind the words.

One-pointed attention is important in daily living because if you don't practice it, you're missing out on *living*, and you're going through your days by rote, repeating what you did the previous day. Before you know it you're wondering what happened to your life? Where did all the time go? You need to keep your mind in the present to fully appreciate the gifts and opportunities that each day offers.

Not fully experiencing the present can be a very subtle form of mental sabotage. As an experiment, next time you're washing the dishes or working on the car, notice how often your mind wanders. Suddenly it takes a hop, skip, and a jump to the argument you had with your son yesterday, and then another jump to that raise your boss promised but still hasn't given. Those wandering thoughts are very skilled at distracting you from matters at hand. You may *think* that you're working on getting your carburetor lid off, or getting the grease off last night's dinner plates, but underneath all that are these whispers of other things that may be on your mind. Once you become aware of where your thoughts *really* are, you become aware of these subtle "tapes" that play, and you can make a conscious effort to say "Stop!" and bring your mind back to what you're doing at hand, thereby shifting your focus from past and future to the present.

I am not a morning person, but to take care of some extra work, I began to wake up one to two hours earlier in the mornings. One morning in particular, as I sat on my back porch taking a coffee break and thinking about all the things

I had to do during the rest of that day, all of a sudden thought: Whoa! Wait a minute. This is *my* time. Why am I thinking about all the things I have to do a few hours from now? Those activities aren't pertinent at six o'clock in the morning! So I sat still and listened to the quiet of my neighborhood at that early hour. A breeze came up and I took a deep breath of the intoxicating summer smells. I made a conscious decision to simply enjoy the moment and not think about anything past or future. I felt completely peaceful and, for the first time, thoroughly enjoyed just existing—I felt truly alive and enjoyed who I was and where I was. I didn't worry about the bills that had to be paid, the traffic I would encounter on the way to work, what to prepare for dinner that night. I looked at the sunlight filtering through the trees and watched the birds flying from branch to branch. I just let myself be, and I felt a surge of love and contentedness course through me, the depth of which I'd never felt before. Once I realized how much and how often my thoughts were headed toward things and people not in the present, I began to feel robbed of my time in the here and now. I was missing out on things that were happening all around me, because I was seeing things only with my normal eyes, and not with the eyes of my heart and with my mind and was too preoccupied by the past, which I couldn't change, and the future, which was yet to happen.

Developing one-pointed attention is a skill that requires practice. We have to train our minds to pay complete attention to the task at hand and to our immediate surroundings. This is not as easy as it sounds in today's world, where you're judged and valued by the number of things you can do simultaneously. We rarely do one thing at a time anymore—we drive our cars while talking on car phones or listening to the radio; we eat lunch while reading the newspaper; students do their homework with music blaring and the television on. No wonder we sometimes have a hard time remembering what we did five minutes ago! We are so busy leading scattered lives, we are neglecting ourselves and living in fantasies of what should be, memories of what was, and expectations of what could be.

To live distractedly means we have been running from something, such as our fears of feeling inadequate, lonely, and angry. If we stop and listen and focus on the present moment, we will have stopped running and will see how we have lived our lives in fear and according to others' expectations. Being in the here and now, being truly awake to our bodies, our fears, our feelings of worthiness, and challenge takes courage. A wonderful thing happens when we face our own pain and suffering: we realize that we are not alone.

One-pointed attention is imperative for learning, remembering, and proper listening. If your child is explaining something to you and you're not focused on what's being said, that child can feel the difference. By not fully focusing, you are telling the child that listening is not all that important. Then, when the child yells "Mom! You're not *listening* to me," you apologize, listen to what's being said, and then perhaps make up for not listening in the first place by buying her something to alleviate your guilt.

There is no substitute for undivided attention. Children know.

Here are some tips on doing one task at a time:

• When washing dishes, don't think about the argument you had with an old friend ten years ago. Instead, focus on the circular motion of the sponge on the pots, the water on your hands, and all the suds. Enjoy the present moment.

- When driving, concentrate on the road and the other drivers. Pay attention to what's on the road around you, not what's playing on the radio, what you have to do tomorrow, or whom you could call on your cellular phone. Enjoy the present moment.
- When someone walks up to you to tell you something, drop what you're doing and give that person your undivided attention: look into his eyes; turn your body fully toward him, not just partway; listen to him with your body, eyes, ears, and mind. Enjoy the moment.

You will notice something incredible. All of a sudden, the present moment will become incredibly heightened: Colors will look brighter, and sound will be clearer. You will not need to put the volume on the television so high because your attention will be fully focused on what you're watching and by tuning in to what's being played out in front of you, you will be able to hear everything more clearly than ever before.

To help you experience your life on a moment-to-moment basis through one-pointed attention, refer to chapter 8 on meditation and chapter 9 on mantras and affirmations. It's worth the effort. You're worth the effort!

16

Comfort Zones: Seeing the Buddha in the Neon Lights

Working toward a spiritual life in the late twentieth century is admittedly difficult. It's not comfortable, and it's not meant to be comfortable. The sense of peace that people have spent lifetimes searching for—and some, like Buddha, Gandhi, and Jesus, have found—is a oneness with ourselves and with those around us—animals and man, and the Earth on which we live. It's about acceptance, tolerance, compassion, understanding, and love.

Inner serenity and peace is not about walking around with a big smile, greeting everyone with open arms, and calling them "brother" and "sister." We are here on this Earth to find our connectedness to the one spiritual being. Whether we call that being God, Allah, Father, or Great Spirit, the essence is still the same. It takes dedication to constantly put our good intentions into daily practice, to stay on the middle path of life, or on the red road, as the path is called in the Native American tradition.

Even with the current trend of living in a more natural way, such as growing vegetables in gardens, making homemade breads and cakes and cooking meals from scratch instead of microwaving frozen boxes, and working closer to home or even *at* home to be closer to children and families, there is still a strong current of our society that seems to be caught up in a materialistic way of life, perpetuating the view that an item or service has worth only if there is a brand name attached to it and if it is sold for, usually, an inordinate amount of money. Truth, values, knowledge, and love don't cost any money, but the price we pay for ignoring these elements in ourselves and those around us is much too high.

A neat trick we have all developed to keep the truth and love in ourselves at bay is to surround ourselves with comfort zones. These zones help buffer our inner selves from feelings of loneliness and inadequacy that crop up sometimes when we feel we've been neglected, or were forced to face something that makes us uncomfortable—something we may not want to face completely.

A comfort zone is a protective shield we wear when we don't face ourselves and our lives fully and refuse to take responsibility for our actions. The key word here is *responsibility*. People like to play the victim and blame everything that happens to them on God, fate, bad luck, or on others. Some people seek out comfort zones every day. Life is hard work, and we make comfort zones our reward.

So what exactly is a comfort zone? It's that cigarette we have when we're upset; it's the pint of chocolate ice cream we eat after we've broken up with somebody; it's the beer or shot of whiskey we have at the end of every day to "relieve" the day's tension; it's the shopping spree we go on when we're feeling down about ourselves. Comfort zones are things we do, or turn to, that make us feel comfortable and secure in times of insecurity or emotional pain.

Comfort zones can be created by buying luxury items such as expensive jewelry or clothing or by buying everyday items such as cigarettes and food. Comfort zones can also be sustained by repeating feel-good memories from childhood.

Food, a major comfort zone for many people, has a strong tie to childhood. I'm not talking about the necessary foods that we must eat to maintain our health, but about that pint of ice cream we eat if a date hasn't gone well; the chocolate cake or cookies devoured in a sitting if we have an argument with a family member or friend. How many of us, as children, were offered some kind of food as solace if we were upset? The goodies were given to us with the assurance, "Here, this will make you feel better."

There's nothing wrong with seeking comfort when we're feeling down, but it shouldn't become a full-time race away from the real reasons we may be hurt or feeling down. If we resort to eating or drinking or smoking to ease any discomfort we feel, that means we're not dealing with what's bothering us. While comfort zones aren't always bad things, they can become counterproductive when we let them run our lives.

There's nothing wrong with eating ice cream or cookies in moderation, and for the right reasons! I cannot stress this enough. Whether it's food or cigarettes, we have been mistrained to turn to outside sources for the comfort that will make us feel better. What we have to remember is that after that cigarette is smoked and the plate of pie is eaten, the argument or the problem is still there. It hasn't gone away just because we stopped thinking about it temporarily. Our problems can be solved only from within ourselves. We have to take responsibility for our actions, and not just sit back and think that the next person will clean up our messes. People always have something to complain about, and when they're asked why they don't tackle the issues that trouble them, they often say "Oh, well, I don't have time," or, "I don't know how," or "What difference can I, one person, make?" We have become a nation of armchair activists waiting for others to do our work for us. We need to lower our level of comfort both as a society and as individuals if we are to make any kind of difference and live full lives.

If you complain about too many pesticides being used on vegetables, then start your own organic vegetable plot. If you don't have space, talk to someone else in your neighborhood who might be able to help you, and maybe even start a community garden. There! Now you've stopped complaining and have become active in taking responsibility for your own life.

Our own obsessive desires represent our greatest source of suffering. Have you ever thought about why we always seem to be in such a state of emotional ambivalence between what we feel we should do and what we actually do? We create this problem and feed our inner struggles and insecurities, through our determination to be right at any cost and through our stubbornness and resistance to anything that challenges our belief system.

When life goes the way we like it to, we're up, happy, and vibrating highly. When our beliefs are questioned, challenged, or shaken, we become distraught, defensive, and depressed. Then we enter a comfort zone and stick our heads in the sand. We become defensive and blame other people and situations, and refuse to take responsibility ourselves. Things don't just happen to us. We create all our own experiences by the way we react to the circumstances we encounter. We tend to expect life to give us what we want before we earn it.

Our strength will come only when we look at every situation, good or bad, as a learning experience. It will come only when we take responsibility for our negative reactions and the old habits we've been holding on to for fear of change and consequent loss of self.

Comfort zones can be broken down only when we face our inner struggles and stop pampering our egos with rewards. Stop the nonsense! Let's stop playing games with ourselves. Stop the mental Ping-Pong game between the ego and the true self.

It's okay to let go!

17

Anger

We've all experienced anger. Some of us even enjoy it! Anger, an impediment to spiritual growth, can take many forms— shouting, violence, curt responses and clipped tones, smoking, shopping, overeating, undereating, drinking, and taking drugs, among others.

Where does all our anger come from? If we take a close look at this powerful emotion, we'll find that a lot of our anger actually stems from fear of not being able to control the outcome of a situation or the actions of another person. It stems from our not accepting a situation or the way a person is acting because it is different from the way that *we* would act, and we don't understand why they can't do it *our* way. Sometimes, for the angry person, anger carries a fulfilling sense of feeling alive. The heart races, breathing becomes rapid, and the anger seems to create energy. I used to enjoy my anger because it made me feel as though all of my nerves were sizzling and ready for action. There was excitement in the air! But I realized that there are more productive ways to feel alive than through anger, and that the ramifications of wanting to feel more of this particular emotion rather than less of it were not altogether healthy for me—mentally or physically. Anger is an acceptable emotion if someone has wronged you or made you feel inferior. Anger can be a good thing if the situation or person has stepped into your personal boundaries and belittled you or caused you harm in some way. Anger can also work to your benefit if it helps you avoid playing the victim and take control over a situation.

Most often, we blame other people and situations for making us so angry. How many times have you said to someone, "You make me so mad!"? The other person didn't make you mad—you made yourself mad, possibly because you felt that the way the person acted was not the way you would have acted if you were the other person. Therefore, the person is wrong. This thought may be confusing because it is *very* subtle and mainly goes unnoticed in our conscious minds. A typical example of how our anger can be based on control can be seen in this not unusual utterance: "I can't believe she did that. She makes me so mad. If I were her, I would have . . ."

We have become a people who fear rather than accept those who are different from us. It's a vicious circle we've created and must learn how to break. If a person acts or looks different, we categorize and pigeon-hole him and say that he's wrong for acting or dressing a certain way. However, we're not really angry at that person for being different, so much as envious that he feels free enough to be himself. He's not afraid to dress differently, to handle a situation differently, to be exactly who he is and immune to our control.

We are a predictable species, but we are also all different. Each of us has our own quirks that mark our individual personality. But somehow, we still expect our children to be "just like us," and when they're not, and they develop their own opinions about things, we become angry and say such things as "You're not my kid. I don't know where you get your ideas from. You're not like your father or me." What are we getting at and why are we really angry?

Did the child commit a crime, or did the child just express views that are different from ours? (In some families, the latter *is* a crime!) We try to teach a child to stand on her own two feet, but by giving her these confusing verbal messages, what we're really saying is "You can be independent and have your own opinions, but make sure those opinions match ours." We have to accept people for who they are and let them be who they feel they need to be.

Anger can stem from fear, insecurity, jealousy, and envy. We get angry at other people because somewhere, deep down in our psyche, unconsciously, we see them doing something we've always wanted to do and, for one reason or another, haven't done. So instead of celebrating their success, we put them down because we can't accept the anger we feel at ourselves for not having followed through on our own dreams and desires. Bottom line: We have traded in the freedom of being ourselves and allowing ourselves simply to *be* for society's stringent do's and don'ts. By facing our anger and its true source, we can come face to face with our own inadequacies.

Taking responsibility for our anger and our actions, and being truly honest about our emotions are the keys to finding happiness within ourselves, and the best things we can ever do for ourselves. Consider it a long-term investment. Take responsibility for your feelings and your anger instead of blindly blaming others.

To ensure inner happiness and peace, we need to learn where our anger stems from and honestly examine that source. What we discover about ourselves does not have to be confessed on a soapbox in the middle of the living room or in the cafeteria at work. It can be quietly admitted internally, in a moment of reflection, and need never be spoken of.

Here's a situation for you: An old classmate from college (opposite sex) has been keeping in touch with your spouse, and you know deep down it's nothing more than a friendship, yet you find yourself still getting angry with your spouse for talking to that person and keeping up the friendship. Of course, you'll never say it in so many words, but little digs are enough. Are you angry at your spouse or are you angry with yourself for your reactions because you're insecure about yourself or your relationship? Are you jealous of the friendship? If you discover where your anger truly stems from and give it its proper place, you've taken the first step toward living a more relaxed life.

Nobody is responsible for you or your actions except *You*. Sometimes the action or word that sets off your anger in the first place is not the real reason for it. Maybe it's really something else that's been glowing just beneath the surface of your emotions, safely buried until something said in all innocence fans your rage into flames. When this happens, the best thing to do is to jump right into the middle of that anger. You may be quite surprised to learn where your anger is coming from and even how long it's been there inside you!

Okay, so now you have an idea as to why you get angry, but what can be done to stop what usually ends up looking like a mental train wreck? The answer: acceptance and understanding. Why are you angry and annoyed at having to stand in a long line at the bank on a Saturday morning? Because you have *so many things to do*. But do you *have* to do everything on that particular morning? No, but you *want* to so you won't have to do anything during the week, leaving you with more free time to do other things. And as you stand there in line, impatiently watching the teller who seems to be taking too much time with each transaction, you get angry because of the time you're wasting by waiting. Now try looking at the situation a little differently: The teller may be taking longer than you would like, but he's doing his job. He's making sure the transactions are being properly handled and he's sorting the right amount of money. Don't you want that same careful attention paid to your account when it comes to your turn?

We cause a lot of our own anger, though we may not realize it. We need to take a step back and realize where all this anger is coming from. There is so much to learn from this fiery emotion, and a great way to deal with it is to constantly question it and try to discover within ourselves why we feel so angry at a particular person or situation. We must follow each answer we learn with another "why?" until we finally get to the root of our emotion. Once we've answered our *whys*, what's the next step?

Well, we can either ignore our realizations and continue to get angry and possibly have to deal with ulcerous conditions (and not many friends), or we can let go of our desire for control, no matter how unconscious it is, by admitting that we can't control certain things. There's nothing we can do about how others think and act, and, regardless of whether we accept it or not, we're going to have to deal with certain people and situations that can and will get us angry, so why not let go of anger's hold?

If we don't let it go, our anger may increase, turn inward and can eventually manifest itself as physical illnesses.

Another important point to remember is that it's okay to not *understand* a particular relationship or situation, but it is imperative for us to understand that we can't change it. Whether we call it karma, fate, or the process of living and learning, each of us must try saying to ourselves: "I don't understand that relationship, there's nothing I can do to change it, so I'm letting it go."

If we find that our anger is powered by insecurity, or jealousy (which is insecurity in disguise), we must work toward changing it. Even the admission—quietly, and to ourselves—as to why we react the way we do in certain circumstances, is the beginning of change.

When I wrote earlier about anger that simmers in you without your knowing it until an off-hand remark tips it off, I was talking about misplaced anger. Suppose a friend or coworker says something to you and you hit the roof. What are you really angry at? It may not be what the person *said* at all, but the *tone* of how it was said. It might have triggered something within you and reminded you of the way your father or ex-husband or even a teacher used to talk to you and belittle you in a certain tone of voice. So your anger is really stemming from an unresolved situation in the past, rather than from the one at hand.

How do you resolve misplaced anger? Confront the source of your original anger. Even if the person you're really angry at doesn't respond in an accepting manner, at least you were able to talk to the person about it. Get it out of your system. If you have anger left over from a past situation and there's no way to confront the person who was involved, try writing a letter, pouring out all of your feelings as honestly as possible, and, instead of actually sending the letter, burn it, setting free all the confining emotions that have bound you for so long. Also, as you burn the letter, ask for forgiveness from the other person, for the other person, for yourself, and ask for healing from the guiding spirits. This is a powerful ritual and helps shift your anger at people and unresolved situations back to the proper place. It also helps you to let go of the past. By letting go of the past, you are free to move on with the present and the future.

18

Trying to Smell the Flowers
in a Concrete Garden

One of my vacations recently was a visit to my parents in Arizona. Originally from the East Coast, my family's westward migration began when my oldest brother moved to Hawaii, and a short time later my other brother settled in California. Not long ago, my parents finally succumbed to the westward pull, leaving me, the only girl and the youngest in the family, back east. Having grown up on the East Coast, with highways for my backyard and parking lots for my front, the idea of driving three hours through a desert to get to my parents' house from the airport struck me as a delicious idea. So off I went. I didn't realize at the start of my drive that being in the desert and seeing the mountains everywhere would have a more powerful effect on me than I would have thought possible.

Upon arriving in the Cactus State, I understood how much I had become accustomed to the constant East Coast congestion, the huge malls and superstores, and giant parking lots otherwise known as highways. I have always felt that this world is made up of hard, sharp edges and concrete—flowers, trees, and grass are not a natural landscape but merely decorations for all the houses and office buildings. I once knew someone who didn't want to deal with cutting the grass in front of his house, so he had it landscaped with different colored rocks. He was saved from doing the backyard because that was already paved as a huge driveway!

When I arrived at the airport and began my journey through the desert, I actually felt that I was *home* for the first time in my life. My body actually resonated with the breathtaking panorama. It was such a relief to my senses to see the Earth the way it was (and still should be) before men in the white shirts and gray suits decided to pave over everything and build an office or condominium on every available square inch of land. To finally see in person all the shades of brown, red, black, yellow, and tan of the mountains and desert that I had previously seen only in pictures, really made an impression that will stay with me for the rest of my life.

Looking up at the sheer majesty of the mountains, I got the feeling that Mother Earth was secretly laughing at human civilization's belief that it could conquer her. She's just biding her time. In some places, she has already taken back what belongs to her through what we call natural disasters (earthquakes and floods), but what the Earth would call cleaning house.

To survive in this lifetime, not merely physically, but with our emotions and hearts fully open, we must realize that life is not about the JC Penney's white sale or the latest fashion craze, and it's especially not about the latest gossip of who did what to whom. Life is about caring for one another, sometimes at the sacrifice of our own comfort. We need to work together. This is not an advertisement or a lecture for the "Random Acts of Kindness" slogan we see on billboards and car bumpers everywhere, but it is the truth. Life is about sharing and caring—giving unconditionally. As human beings, we have a responsibility to our society, child and adult, human and animal.

Society has become too caught up in materialism, which in the grand scheme doesn't count for much. So you bought the latest Lexus, and you're proud. Great that you are successful enough in your life to be able to afford such a luxury, but so what? Can you take it with you when you die? Are you truly happy inside of yourself because you own that Lexus? Does it make your family members happy aside from the fact that they can drive everywhere in comfort? Does owning it help your children understand and practice compassion for others?

There's nothing wrong with wanting a better life. That was one of the driving forces that helped settle America and kept people going through the difficult times, but we've become enveloped and lost in our comfort zones. Comfort has become the way of life. Maybe we're tired of fighting and just want to relax, but sometimes that can lead to not living at all. We need to get away from that kind of thinking. We should stop the "Why should I help others when nobody helps me?" syndrome.

In no other time have there been so many people in therapy searching for that elusive "something" that's missing from their lives. That missing something eludes most of us in today's society—it's being in touch with ourselves. Through the media, we've been taught to define ourselves by what we look like and how many and what kind of possessions we own. This materialistic view has been a slow evolution that was whipped up into a frenzied pace in the last century.

Deep down, I believe people realize that money and material possessions cannot make them happy, but we've lived under the sway of false values for so long that we've forgotten what we're all about. We've become a society that lives for instant gratification.

People in our grandparents' and great-grandparents' generation wanted a better life, so they immigrated to this country, worked hard, and acquired a roof over their heads and a steady job to help make life a little easier. People used to work with the Earth by planting and harvesting and living off the land; they didn't treat dirt and falling leaves as a nuisance.

Each successive generation has wanted to do better than the one before it, but people got caught up with materialism and began to get greedy. "A two-bedroom house was good enough for my parents, but I have to have a three-bedroom house," one person says. "We need the luxurious, top-of-the-line, leather interior, walnut dashboard version, so we can ride to work in more comfort, so we can earn more money, so we can buy more things, so we can live more comfortably," thinks another; but when put into actual words it comes out sounding like "We need another car."

There's nothing wrong with having material things if a balanced cycle of giving and taking occurs. The Karmic Law of Life states: You get something and you give something back. Many people have become exclusive takers and we are slowly realizing that the amount of property we own and how we look are no longer enough to fulfill us. We've forgotten that we are supposed to live together as a community on this planet, not just as individuals. But, of course, we always act happy. We smile at public functions and strive to paint a picture that our life is perfect.

Well, you know what? If life is so perfect for you and me with all our quick and easy luxuries, why do we still feel so empty? Most people react to "I'm bored," or "I'm mad" or "I'm sad" by thinking, "Maybe I'll go shopping and I'll feel better." Sure, that will make you happier—for a short while—but then what? You start to feel that emptiness again and then go out and buy something else.

We've gotten too far away from what we're here for. We're here to work together for a better life as a community, not just for ourselves as individuals. We have gotten caught in the net of a materialistic culture.

To be mindful of our soul means to go against modern values. Unfortunately, most people wait until they have a heart attack or ulcers, or until their spouse leaves them or some other life-shattering event occurs before attending to their soul needs. As human beings many of us have forgotten how to play and simply *be*. All the adult stuff that life requires— holding a job, paying bills,—can magnify and finally fill our entire life. There aren't many moments in our lives anymore for us to experience our *souls*. Children experience their souls on a daily basis. You can hear it in their laughter.

Loss of soul creates a void in us, and we fill this emptiness by watching TV or working longer hours. A decision and commitment to reconnect our soul is the same as for any change for the better, whether it's to stop smoking or start eating a healthier diet.

Become aware of how deprived your life is of sources of joy, beauty, and creativity. Find the silent parts of yourself and ask yourself what gave you pleasure as a child that you may not have done for years. Gardening? Fishing? When you recover or discover something that nourishes your soul and brings joy, care enough about yourself to make room for it in your life.

We have all looked for things outside of ourselves to make us happy, to fill us up when we're down, but happiness comes from inside of us. Inner work is what's needed to slow down our depressions and fill the void. Things happen to us, yes, but it is how we react to these events that determines the level of happiness within ourselves and in the world around us. We have free will to choose solutions to our problems. Our problems are not *us*. We mustn't take them personally. Inner peace is what we're after.

Epilogue

We all have commitments of various kinds and to various *others*: to our jobs, our families, our churches and synagogues, our society. But we have a tendency to forget the need to make a commitment to ourselves. We have forgone that particular commitment for the sake of meeting everything and everybody else's needs.

We don't all have the luxury of being able to take a few hours out of each day to replenish our mental health by getting a relaxing massage or taking a yoga class or just sitting in restful meditation for thirty minutes. So we must adapt. We need to.

My goal in offering this book to you is to show you how to combine the two necessities of modern life—juggling work, bills, and family with taking care of yourself. The two tasks needn't be mutually exclusive. In fact, you can't give to others—coworkers, neighbors, or even your own children—if there is little to draw on within your*self*.

We have become a run-down society. Is that why the number of hours people spend in front of the television is so extraordinarily high? We've become a country of couch potatoes.

But you can do something about it. Adapt your current lifestyle to include the breathing exercises, yoga postures, and healthier eating habits. If you feel that even that is too much, you can at least change the way you look at and react to things, by becoming more aware of where your emotions come from, and by treating others with kindness and respect. Imagine how much cleaner the world would be if each person took care of sweeping the area just in front of his or her own house.

What I'm saying is it all begins with us—each individual.

Suggested Reading

Food

The Moosewood Cookbook. Mollie Katzen. Berkeley, Calif.: Ten Speed Press, 1992.

Still Life With Menu. Mollie Katzen. Berkeley, Calif.: Ten Speed Press, 1988.

The Enchanted Broccoli Forest. Mollie Katzen. Berkeley, Calif.: Ten Speed Press, 1982.

The Egg Project. Gary Null. New York: Four Walls Eight Windows, 1987.

The Self-Healing Cookbook. Kristina Turner. Green Valley, Calif.: Earth Tones Press, 1989.

Visualization/Meditation/Inspiration

Be Here Now. Ram Dass. New York: Crown Publishing, 1992.

Climbing the Blue Mountain. Eknath Easwaran. Tomales, Calif.: Nilgiri Press, 1992.

Conquest of Mind. Eknath Easwaran. Tomales, Calif.: Nilgiri Press, 1988.

Creative Visualization. Shakti Gawain. New York: Bantam Books, 1982.

Sacred Manhood, Sacred Earth: A Vision Quest Into the Wilderness of a

Man's Heart. Joseph Jastrab with Ron Schaumburg. New York: HarperPerennial, 1994.

Change Your Life Now: Get Out of Your Head, Get Into Your Life, Gary Null. Deerfield Beach, Fla.: Health Communications Inc., 1993.

A Path With Heart: A Guide Through the Perils and Promises of Spiritual Life. Jack Kornfield. New York: Bantam Books, 1993.

Medical

Encounters With Qi: Exploring Chinese Medicine. David Eisenberg, M.D., with Thomas Lee Wright. New York: W.W. Norton and Company, 1995

The Way of Herbs. Michael Tierra. New York: Simon and Schuster, 1990

Spontaneous Healing. Andrew Weil. New York: Alfred A. Knopf, 1995

Natural Health, Natural Medicine: A Comprehensive Manual for Wellness and Self-Care. Andrew Weil, M.D., Boston: Houghton Mifflin Company, 1990

Bibliography

Anderson, Bob. *Stretching*. Bolinas, Calif.: Shelter Publications, 1980.

Bahm, Archie J. *Yoga for Business Executives and Professional People*. New York: Citadel Press, 1969.

Bauman, Edward, Lorin Piper, Armand I. Brint, and Pamela A. Wright. Berkeley Holistic Health Center, *The Holistic Health Handbook: A Tool for Attaining Wholeness of Body, Mind, and Spirit*. Berkeley, Calif.: And/Or Press, 1978.

Chakravarti, Sree. "Mudras: Healing Finger Postures," *Light of Consciousness: A Journal of Spiritual Awakening* 7, no. 1 (winter 1995).

Cunningham, Scott. *Magical Aromatherapy: The Power of Scent*. Llewellyn Publications.: St. Paul, Minn., 1992.

Diamond, Harvey and Marilyn. *Fit for Life*. Warner Books: 1985.

Easwaran, Eknath. *Take Your Time: Finding Balance in a Hurried World*. Tomales, Calif.: Nilgiri Press, 1994.

Frawley, David. "Mantra: Liberating Consciousness Through Sound," *Light of Consciousness: A Journal of Spiritual Awakening* 7, no. 1 (winter 1995).

Gawain, Shakti. *Creative Visualization*. New York: Bantam Books, 1982.

Hanh, Nhat Thich. "Walking Meditation," *Light of Consciousness: A Journal of Spiritual Awakening* 7, no. 1 (winter 1995)

Integral Yoga Institute, Sri Swami Satchidananada. *Integral Yoga Hatha*. Pomfret Center, Conn.: Integral Yoga (cr) Publications, 1979.

Kulvinskas, Viktoras. *Survival Into the 21st Century: Planetary Healers Manual*. Woodstock Valley, Conn.: 21st Century Publications, 1975.

Tierra, Michael *The Way of Herbs*. New York: Simon and Schuster, 1990.

Index

R

S

T

U

V

W

Y

Yellow and candle meditation, 106
Yellow in color healing, 113
Ylang-lang (essential oil), 34
Yoga, xii
  Bhakti, 42–43
  breathing exercises, 38, 56
  chants, 44–45
  eye exercises, 45
  Hatha, 39, 49–55
  Integral, 41
  joining body and mind, 37

Karma, 41–42
portable postures, 57–58
Raja, 40
Siddha, 82
sun salutation pose, 45–48
Tantra, 40–41
Yoga Journal, ix, 38–39

Z

Zone Therapy (Fitzgerald), 18